# Praise for *Chased from Eden*

"What a gorgeous collection of related stories! Put together, they constitute a kind of novel. The final piece, *A War Bride's Journey*, the longest and most ambitious and moving of the collection, is an extraordinary story. Marguerite Vaillancourt beautifully renders wartime Morocco and the plight of civilians who through no fault of their own are caught up in a war's machinations. Her often lyrical prose is always precise and to the point—not a word is wasted. The critic Cleanth Brooks once noted that Keats's "Ode on a Grecian Urn" was 'history without footnotes.' The same is true of Marguerite Vaillancourt's admirable book."

—Geoffrey Clark
Author of *Two, Two, Lily-White Boys*

D1082139

# CHASED FROM EDEN

## Coming of Age in Morocco

❧

MARGUERITE VAILLANCOURT

*[signature: Marguerite Vaillancourt]*

LGP
A Les Gosses Production

Cover photo of shutters in Oudaiya, Rabat, 2008,
by Christine Vaillancourt, 2008.

Back cover photo of author at Hassan Tower,
by Diane Vaillancourt, 2008.

Vaillancourt Publishing, c/o

    Diane K. Vaillancourt
    849 Almar Ave., #C403
    Santa Cruz, CA 95060
    831.458.3440
    www.chasedfromeden.com


ISBN-10: 0991347005
ISBN-13: 978-0-9913470-0-1

This book is printed on acid-free paper.

*In memory of my brother Jacques Pagès,*
*who was then my constant companion*

# ACKNOWLEDGMENTS

Much gratitude goes to Michele Cooper, who first gave me the confidence to express myself in the English language; to Susan Dodd for her early support of my work; to Geoffrey Clark, who included one of my stories in his anthology of Rhode Island writers, *How the Weather Was*; and to Judith Porter, who encouraged me to put my Moroccan stories into book form.

To my dear niece Andrée Pagès for her insightful and patient editing, to my daughter Diane Vaillancourt for her editorial suggestions and elegant design of the overall production, and to my daughter Christine Vaillancourt for her cover design and painstaking work bringing old family album photographs to life, much love to you three! Working on this book with you was a warm and wonderful experience.

Special thanks to Andrew Vahldieck for his many readings and wise commentary.

# CONTENTS

❧

❧

# CHASED FROM EDEN

Rabat - 1929

⤳

I once lived in a garden, a small but lush Moroccan garden comfortably enclosed by a white-washed stucco wall. My memory of the house in its midst is vague and remote, just a solid structure where I could run every so often for solace. I was five years old.

Few intrusions penetrated my world, but those were reassuring: family grown-ups going in and out the gate, always hurrying; the maid in the morning beating carpets on the balcony or checking my whereabouts; street vendors convening by the kitchen door with their fruit and vegetables, squatting on their haunches, ready for long bargaining sessions, their heavy-laden donkeys waiting patiently by the gate.

Sometimes the vendors brought skinny, cackling chickens strung together by the legs over their shoulders. While the haggling went on, I would watch from command posts in small trees near the wall, slipping down once in a while to tweak the beaks of the bound creatures, taunting them into pecking at my finger. Once in a while a camel awaited its master beyond the gate, munching on leaves and branches from the large mimosa tree hanging over the wall, its upper lip curling to display dirty teeth protruding from a triangular mouth. I kept a safe distance and watched the greenery sway as the ugly beast pulled at it from the outside.

The shrubs in my garden were the perfect height. You could hide in them, or use the sturdier branches to swing from your knees so the world would be upside down. The ground would come and go, brushed by your hair, a most pleasurable feeling. The twisted limbs, like whitish snakes penetrating into thick foliage, would bend under your weight but did not break, adding to the thrill. Bell-like, huge white flowers hung from between the leaves, exuding a sweet scent. These flowers were not to be touched, I had been warned. Very poisonous, they said. You could fall dead, just like that. I touched anyway, but with only one finger. They felt rough and sticky, my first encounter with temptation. Of course I didn't die. Already at that age, still too young to go to school, I was left with the impression that, while not necessarily fatal, the forbidden object can be rather disappointing. Thus the flowers dangled within reach, but safe from destruction.

When somewhat later I first saw a picture of the biblical Eden, I recognized in the landscape my climbing shrubs. The winding snake, the exotic flowers, the lush glossy leaves, all had been part of my garden, which by then belonged to memory since we had moved away. I had no chance to grow older there, and thus that image retained its pristine state forever. No successive layers of added scenes came to encumber the picture, save one, a counter-image that attached itself to the ancient remembrance. Somewhat weaker, a pale reflection of the original, it stripped the landscape of its lushness in one stroke, leaving only a skeleton of snake-like boughs in the now ravished garden, the consequence of an unexpected turn of events upsetting my limited perception of the world.

It happened during a particularly warm day, at siesta time, with no one around. I had stolen a spoon from the kitchen and was secretly digging into the red soil between the bushes, intending to make clay balls to harden in the sun, when I thought I heard the black drummer in the distance. I jumped up, ready to run back to the house for cover. I dreaded the sight of him and knew the sounds of his drum a mile away. He would come by the garden gate arrayed in wild animal skins with strings of fangs and bells covering his chest. If he could catch a small audience, he would perform, chanting and beating on his drum while I cowered behind a safe grown-up presence, prudently out of reach.

But this time the drumbeats sounded different, coming from all over the neighborhood, banging noises, followed by high-pitched yells. I peeked into the street. People had gathered out in the open with kettles and pots, hitting them with sticks. Even Arab women had emerged without their street coverings, with just scarves tied over their heads. They were pointing at the sky. Drawn by the noise, all our household came out too. Above us, a thick cloud the color of tarnished silver was hovering in an otherwise cloudless sky. The banging and yelling reached a crescendo, but to no avail. The cloud spread lower, a widening shadow becoming lighter as it expanded into a myriad of flying creatures. In no time the locusts were swooping down, whirring by, hitting us in their frenzied flight. As we ran into the house for cover, they settled in copper and green waves on the trees, the grounds, the walls, hitting the windowpanes as we watched. By then, most noises from the street had subsided, giving in to the invasion.

The next morning we ventured out. Using an umbrella to fend off the remainder of the flying insects, my mother took me down the steps over a carpet of dead ones. We tiptoed gingerly, crunching them as we walked. In death they had blackened, the live ones crawling over them. My garden was gone, stripped but for the serpentine branches and bits of white flowers on which a few creatures still munched.

Gone! A bright sun shone through bare trees onto the dark ground as we ran toward the street, sickened by the sight.

Eventually, the garden came back to life. But it did not feel the same, ever.

The black drummer did indeed appear soon afterwards. One morning I heard the drumbeats, and this time I knew it was he. His slow progression up the street filled me with the usual anticipation, a mixture of awe and dread, and this time I was not let down. He stopped by the gate and, seeing me there, sauntered in to the beat of his drum. The noise brought my mother out of the house.

He was in full regalia, lion's skin over his shoulders, amulets and fangs on his chest. He started moving his body, slowly at first, then faster, until all parts were shaking as he beat on the long drum. Only his feet stayed still. He seemed very old, with white tufts of frizzy hair sticking out of a turban adorned with feathers. His bare legs looked like twisted logs. All at once, he crouched and leaped like an animal, then danced round and round and round, one arm toward the sky, yelling strange things, only to stop suddenly, and in numbing silence, thrust a gnarled hand toward us, bridging the space between us. I saw his long, desiccated fingers crisscrossed with embedded dirt.

To this day, I do not know why I did it: could it be that temptation and revulsion share common ground? But I rushed toward him and kissed his hand, quickly retreating in confusion. I hope my mother recovered enough to give him a few coins.

Soon after, we moved away.

*Arrival in Rabat with Grandmother, 1927*

*Harbor on Bou Regreg river from high walls of
Oudaiya, Rabat, 1927*

*Bell-like datura arborea blooms*

*Donkeys on road, Marrakesh, 1928*

*With Maman in Marrakesh, 1928*

*Maman by Hassan Tower, Rabat, 1928*

*With Papa in the field surrounding Hassan Tower*
*Rabat, 1928*

*Old minaret in Chellah, our playground*

*With Fatima, Rabat, 1928*

*New house in country outside Rabat, 1934*

*Twelve years old with piano, 1936*

# THE PRINCE

## 1930-1936

∾

Do you know that when I was five and six and seven I had a real prince for a friend? Not an imaginary prince, but one you could touch, who claimed to be a direct descendant of Prophet Mohammed and who was as handsome as a prince should be. Until I met him, my world had been filled with the other kind, surrealistic and vaporous creatures filling skies and other enchanted places. This one was flesh and bone. He did not have to wear princely clothes or Arab robes. Always in a white suit, he stood taller than anybody I knew, his light green eyes, lighter than his tanned skin, giving him an imperious look. He wore a big gold ring adorned with a black scarab on his index finger, while the other hand gripped at all times a chiseled wood and silver cane.

I would loudly welcome his impromptu visits to our house by rushing toward him and hugging his knees, waiting impatiently until he sat down to settle at his feet. Never importuned by my behavior, he would occasionally tweak my cheeks while talking to my father. Once in a while, when I least expected it, he would pull out of his pocket a tiny gift, right in the middle of their conversation, and hand it to me silently. He won me a thousand times over, but my vociferous affection knew no limit on the day he took me along with my brother to the circus. Sitting beside him on the bleachers, I felt the excitement of watching wild animals, an excitement heightened by his presence, which spelled mystery, adventure, and daring. He made us pay special attention to the trained horses. We knew he loved horses, and that a nervous Arabian had thrown him and nearly broken his back long ago.

The mystery spread to his surroundings. His house, a square pavilion with arched windows and scalloped trim giving it a Moorish flavor, was hidden in what seemed at the time an immense garden surrounded by a high red clay wall. He lived there with a strange-looking wife who never seemed to leave the house. She was always dressed in old-fashioned clothes with numerous strands of beads at her neck and long, dangling earrings, looking perplexed at the world around her. They had three handsome and haughty children, nearly all grown by the time we knew them, who ignored me totally. Still I was much impressed when the youngest bragged to me that their mother was Russian, although I had no inkling of what it meant.

The garden was so large I once became lost in it after wandering away from a reception at their house.

My mother was there looking beautiful in her new dress. My non-musical father had been asked to say a few words about Chopin to the assembled guests. It was strange to see my father standing by the grand piano in the middle of the drawing room and talking about this Monsieur Chopin. My friend's wife, the Russian lady, sat down and started playing. She played and played, swaying with the music. After yawning a few times, I could not stay still any longer and managed to escape my mother's side. During a particularly loud piece, I found an open door to the terrace and sneaked into the main alley leading away from the house.

Some flowers I had seen earlier beckoned me to smell them. I took a side path looking for them. But as I searched, the path became smaller and soon disappeared. Dark thickets closed in on me. When I tried to turn around, the maze of glossy bushes held me prisoner. Prickly and threatening, they were heavy with moist and evil-smelling, bell-shaped blooms. Stumbling about, hopelessly lost, I started to whimper, wondering when (or if) my mother would miss me. Faint piano sounds could still be heard, then clapping, then silence.

Lost forever, I cried. I knew I was going to die. Nobody would ever find me.

After what seemed an eternity, distant voices, then laughter, reached my ears. I cried louder. An ominous snapping noise made me freeze; a wild beast was about to pounce. I saw flashes of white, and suddenly here was my friend emerging from the bushes. Following him was my mother in her yellow chiffon gown and new pearl necklace. She hugged me and scolded me gently, laughing at my tears while he wiped away the wet streaks on my face with a scented handkerchief. Then he took my hand and led me back to the house, where he asked his daughter to let me play with the Russian dolls.

Walking was usually the way our family got around the new city that was rising outside the confines of the medina. We often took the path along my prince's property, now wedged between new construction and wide, open avenues. The red stucco walls surrounding his gardens stretched endlessly while the sun beat down on us. I could see the top of his trees over the wall, but their foliage gave us no relief from the heat, just the promise of cool shade on the other side. The dust from the baked earth would lift with each step and cover my shoes. Trailing along behind grown-ups who always walked too fast, I would complain out loud to no one in particular, but send silent messages to him: *Don't you know that I am nearby? Can't you tell that I am right here?*

Then finally I would beg: "Why can't we stop and see him?"

"No, not now, some other time," my mother would say, eager to return to grown-up talk. My father would add: "He is probably not at home anyway. But he should be getting in touch with us soon."

The wall would turn abruptly at a right angle,

hiding away the enchanted park. And just as abruptly, a short time later, my friend would reappear at our door for a brief and joyful moment.

Now I am a little older and I have not seen him for quite a while. Then one day, I am hurrying with the family, this time to the beach. Again we are walking to get there. I hear the surf beating on the rocks and smell the sea spray in the air. I can't wait to get close to the water. Looming high over the walkway is a small white fortress with no windows, only a few slits in its stone walls. I overhear the word "prison" along with my friend's name.

"Is he really there? Inside? But why are they keeping him? What for?"

"Hush, girl, no one really knows. He'll be out soon. Some kind of mix-up… He'll be out soon, you'll see."

From that day on, I never like that beach. While swimming in the surf, it is too hard to ignore the fort-like structure above with its slits for windows. Unnoticed before, it remains linked with the stench of the tide…

Eventually he was let out. How soon afterwards, I can't remember. One Sunday morning while skipping rope in the public park under my grandmother's watchful eye, I saw him walking by with his wood and silver cane, as dashing as ever in his white silk suit. He was limping slightly. With my brother at my heels, I rushed into his open arms. He had trouble bending over, so we climbed on a nearby bench and he clutched us to his chest. When he released us, we whooped with joy, running circles around him.

After that his visits tapered off and became less memorable. He might have been under police surveillance. I was too young to understand what the problem was. Moreover I was growing up and my affections were shifting away. Overt admiration for anyone real became subdued, even repressed: I had discovered books! In reading Sir Walter Scott and Jack London I found other heroes, letting my imagination run wild in the misty landscapes of Scotland and the wild coasts of Alaska even as, under a calmer demeanor, I learned to curtsey in front of visitors.

From time to time, I would still think of my friend. By then, he had retreated to an estate he owned in the back country. My family made one attempt to visit him there, but the roads were treacherous and halfway there we had to turn back. In town, the modern avenues slicing away the enchanted garden finally revealed an empty and abandoned house.

News of his sudden death, in my teens, caught me breathless. I had always expected to see him again, and the finality of forever-broken bonds distressed me deeply. Who was he really that we had once been so attracted to him? Had he truly cared for us as well?

The frail-looking widow received us with frightened eyes in a darkened parlor: "Alas, alas," she would only say. A sparsely attended and hurried funeral followed in a Moslem cemetery. Only men could be present.

When my father returned home and, lost in thought, finally settled down, I approached him gently: "What did you really know about him?"

I half expected the answer. "Very little, I'm afraid. We met by chance at a cafe in Fez when your mother and I first arrived in the country, and we never quite understood why he sought out our company. He certainly was a favorite of yours, wasn't he?"

I nodded. He went on: "I suspect he was a mystery even to himself. A family man, no doubt, a businessman and landowner. To many of his people, he may have been a patriot defying French authority; also an adventurer, an informer perhaps, all of the above—but maybe not, who knows? He could very well have been a descendant of Mohammed, as he had always claimed."

"But his Russian wife, how did he meet her?"

My father smiled. "Long ago, as a young man, he lived in Italy. He even became an officer in their cavalry. Can you just picture him in the kind of uniform they wore in those days?"

I savored the image. The first line of a poem by Apollinaire came to me: *"Bel officier, couleur du ciel..."* What could be more dashing than the trappings of an Italian cavalry officer at the turn of the century, the plumes, the tassels, the light blue uniform and perfectly obedient but skittish mount? How handsome he must have looked!

"He met his wife in Florence, where she was vacationing with her family; a little Russian countess, so he told us. His regiment was stationed downstream on the Arno River. It was love at first sight, at a garden party. He wooed her in French, their only common language. Her father viewed the match with misgivings, yet but she would have nobody but him. After many tears, she won. She was very young and very spoiled. After it was pointed out that the young man was a prince, her family gave in."

I begged my father to go on. You see, I was at the right age to love the story, so fitting for my friend.

"Well, they were married, and after a long honeymoon in a family dacha, they lived in St. Petersburg, where he held some honorary post as a military attaché. In those days Russia put few obstacles in the path of true love and influential fathers-in-law. But the city's cold skies and the boorishness of its inhabitants soon depressed him. He would tell me how he used to go horseback riding around the flat and frozen countryside and how dismal the scenery looked to him. Even the woods had a lifeless quality, dotted as they were with the pale trunks of birches reminding him of straight, giant worms. He yearned for the rocky and luminous landscapes of his Moroccan homeland, where sky and earth collided, blue on top of red, and where almond trees bloomed before winter was over. He was disturbed by the sullen looks of the peasants, who with obsequious bows lowered their eyes at his passage. He remembered the open simplicity of his countrymen..."

I nodded. In Morocco even the poorest carried themselves with dignity. "Did they leave then?"

"Yes, he soon convinced his young wife to go with him to the sunny and hospitable land of his ancestors" —I could hear the prince using those same words— "where he owned considerable property. Ominous signs of impending war in Europe overcame the objections of her father, who let her go, never to see her again. She brought along a very bulky piano, two samovars, and her large collection of dolls..."

I remembered the dolls in dusty lace with pale porcelain faces, the peasant dolls in babushkas, the bride dolls dressed in red, all displayed in disarray on a long bench under the main hall window.

"After arriving in Morocco, she gave birth to their first child. Soon their family increased. It was now her turn to pine for her homeland, for a Russia that was no more. She did not care for the sun and lived behind closed shutters, playing her beloved Chopin. Evidently they went through hard times as some of their land was confiscated for lack of papers showing ownership. Then he was suspected of selling arms to rebel tribes in the mountains. But there was no proof. So the authorities detained him for a while, then let him go. He did not fit any mold and likely remained as much of a mystery to them as he was to us. But they kept hounding him."

As I turned to leave, my father kissed me on the forehead: "A little sad, isn't it?"

I wouldn't answer, but just went to my room. The evening air, when I opened the window, was heavy with the fragrance of the mimosa trees then in bloom. On his first night in the ground, I called silently to him one last time: *My friend, my prince, you are free now...*

# VILLA BLANCHE

## 1932

✥

When I was eight, my family moved to a house called Villa Blanche, more room being needed due to the impending arrival of a third child. At the time I was blissfully unaware of that fact, but very happy that my beloved grandmother had traveled all the way from France to Morocco for the occasion.

Added to the joy of having her among us was the instant affinity I felt for our new home. Aptly named for its white stucco walls, with long narrow windows and dark green shutters, situated on a corner lot, the villa was a tall, imposing structure partly hidden from the street behind a huge eucalyptus tree. The house breathed mystery, with its multilevel floors ending in a tower-like room at the very top. I suspect our father had intended to use this room as a refuge from us all, to read and write in peace, but since it was not locked we felt free to make it our playground when he was not around. Anyway, he soon abandoned the idea of a place for solitude as he also liked maintaining control over his family, and when meals were done he would install himself in the dining room, so dark it always needed artificial light even on the brightest days. Here I did my homework in his presence.

But the vantage point of the room on top was exhilarating for somebody my age. From a single window you could look down onto the rear courtyard with all its activities, see the chicken coop, the laundry area, the empty horse stalls that would later shelter our first car. For reasons of safety we children were strictly forbidden to open that window, but we did anyway, and it was a thrill to bend over the sill and look straight down until you got dizzy. Unseen, you could watch the goings-on of the household far below, the maid, the peddlers and their merchandise, my always harried mother going back and forth outside the dungeon-like kitchen half buried in the ground. Looking over beyond the horse stalls, you could see flat rooftops among trees, and to the left, across a small street, a park filled with colorful and unfamiliar vegetation.

To me at age eight the house seemed old. It had probably been built at the beginning of the French protectorate some twenty years earlier, in all likelihood for a cavalry officer and his retinue, hence the horse stalls.

There was so much to explore at first, so many rooms, so many recesses, even a small balcony off my very first own room. The garden had its own attractions: trees easy to climb, bushes in which one could hide, an unused horse trough perfect for experiments. It was summertime when we moved in, and my seven-year-old brother and I combed through the overgrown garden in search of adventure with no need of other companionship. At times Jacques and I did not even seek each other's presence until mealtime brought us to the house, dirty, disheveled, and worn out from our endeavors. The fascination the house held increased even further when he scratched a small spot on the stucco wall in the hall. Suddenly some fine red sand poured out, which convinced him that the whole structure could fall on us at any time. This did not seem believable to me, but I rather enjoyed the prospect of imminent danger.

Around then our little sister was born. It was so very hot, that August afternoon. My mother was sitting outside in the shade and I was playing at her feet when suddenly my grandmother said she would take us to the seashore, a rare event considering that we had to take two buses, hire a boatman to row us to the other side of the river, and then walk half a mile to reach the beach.

When we returned home late that afternoon, our mother was gone, ostensibly to fetch us a new baby. It took her the longest time! Jacques and I were told she had to wait in order to pick the perfect baby out of a boatload coming from France to Casablanca. Of course we swallowed the story, but we honestly could not understand what the big fuss was all about when a few days later we finally saw what was brought home under wraps. We were sitting on the garden wall when the cab arrived, the usual horse-drawn carriage, my father holding the newborn and my mother carrying a big package of pastries. We rushed toward them with happy anticipation and had a peek at the red and wrinkled little face between the covers. It was a big disappointment. So we dismissed her existence rather quickly and instead attacked the goodies with great gusto.

Soon afterwards, I discovered by chance that my grandmother was packing her suitcases and realized she was going back to France. I found out that she was also taking my brother, my only play companion. In those days parents kept children in the dark about their decisions, and I was silently devastated. Finally it was explained to me that the trip was for Jacques' health and that in the following year we would go to France on vacation and bring him back. I was jealous: it should have been me going with her. I wished from the bottom of my heart that I could be fragile too.

They left and my father sulked, mourning the absence of his son, while my mother busied herself with my new baby sister. I made myself scarce, increasingly bored even with the new house.

But summer was ending and soon school started. From the new house it now took me two city bus rides to reach the Lycée de Jeunes Filles, where I had gone before. It was a long trip, too far to return home for lunch as before, and so I stayed there all day. Yet more changes were in store. After three months in school, I was suddenly removed during the Christmas holidays.

I did not understand why, since I was a good student, continuously egged on to be the head of the class by both teachers and parents. Always eager to please, I had done my best to comply. But my father had now decided to take care of my education himself and, being obedient, I did not protest.

Not having a pesky younger brother around, often annoying with his disruptive ways but still a constant companion in invented games, I welcomed my father's undivided attention and the start of the unorthodox education I would receive at home. The first morning, in the early hours before he went to work, I was up and ready to receive my first daily assignment by the dining room table. I sat down to the task with my best resolutions. He was going to be so proud of me!

When I was much younger and barely able to read, my imagination had been stirred when Papa taught me a verse by the avant-garde poet Guillaume Apollinaire to recite in front of company. The lines spurred me to write down my own view of the world, filling a whole page. Since 'heaven' and 'sky' are the same word in French, the fantastic mingled with the prosaic and the real and unreal mixed happily in vivid pictures that I still remember. My parents seemed delighted at the time, perhaps thinking I was precocious, since my brother, just a year younger, was still having trouble writing single letters of the alphabet on lined paper. But my feat was never to be repeated, and I suspect my father felt that going to school had dulled my senses, and thus his decision to take my education in hand.

So on my very first morning, I sat down in front of

the rather thick *Memoirs of Chateaubriand* to diagram each sentence into its components, phrases, clauses, etc... The assignment was over my head—understandably so, if one is familiar with Chateaubriand's prose. I was, after all, only eight.

Although I came to dread those exercises, my imagination was stirred by the writings and the unknown horizons they opened. Chateaubriand had explored the frontiers of the New World when it was still wild and full of virgin forests and Indians. Many words escaped me, but I felt the mystery of his discoveries, his views on the simple "savages," mostly good but at times cruel. He described a river that had no equal in the world, the "Meschacebe," the mysterious Mississippi whose source and outlets were still unknown. I cried at the story of Atala, the Indian maiden whose mother on her deathbed made her promise to become a Christian and remain a virgin. She was in love with a young Indian brave and killed herself to stay faithful to her vows. I could not quite fathom the problem, really; couldn't they all live happily together? But I relished the story and cried many times over the death scene. Only much later I found out that Chateaubriand's descriptions were often borrowed from other travelers and that, French writer that he was, he knew how to stir the imagination of his contemporaries. Yet those facts never erased the imprint he left on my mind of the majesty of the American landscape.

In the afternoon, as long as I kept within hearing distance of my mother, I had nearly complete freedom:

freedom to roam in the garden, to climb trees, to sail my boats in the horse trough. I fashioned a hidden tree-house in a misshapen pine whose trunk had grown horizontally enough to give a nice berth in which to lie and watch the sky. I had no idea of being lonely; it did not cross my mind to miss a girl companion. I essentially enjoyed boyish interests. Sometimes I would be asked to accompany the Arab maid when she took my baby sister in her carriage to the park across the street. I liked the talcum powder smell when I hugged my sister, the embroidered pillow and blanket used for the occasion. Still no children my age were in the park; they were all at school. So the outings were not that enjoyable and I just went as a favor to my mother.

For a while that winter I did have one companion in the garden, a stork as tall as I that followed me around quite faithfully. We kept a respectful distance from one another; she was a little skittish and I was afraid of her long beak. But she would walk behind me, stopping when I stopped, waiting expectantly for the piece of bread that I would have for her. Every morning she would be at the back door waiting until I was let out. When spring came she disappeared suddenly, probably joining a flock returning to Alsace, where they often spent the summer, it was explained to me. I missed her, and to replace the loss, I was given a puppy.

I remember only pleasant evenings. All others, somehow, have left no trace. On rainy or cold nights, once the baby settled down, we would sit around the fireplace in the dining room and read while my mother knitted. Sometimes, Papa would spin tales that took place in strange countries. On clear evenings we would sit out in the garden and watch the stars, which acquired a life of their own when I learned their names. Stars and Greek mythology intertwined in my mind. Sometimes I would walk with my father in the darkened park listening to his stories of the gods' adventures, and they were there, present in the shadows of the bamboo groves, but mindless of us, pursuing their separate fates. I would be awed and enchanted by these tales, while feeling safe at his side.

With springtime came a flurry of preparations for a summer trip to France and the bracing Pyrenees' air. My mother assembled yards of beautiful material bought in the *souks* of the *medina* and had several outfits made by a dressmaker, who took over the dining room for days. Traveling trunks reappeared, slowly filling up. Then carpets were rolled in mothballs and newspapers. Finally shutters were closed tight and an Arab guardian appointed to check the house once in a while. Thus we left Villa Blanche and headed for Casablanca where an ocean liner would take us to France, a trip lasting four or five days—the date of arrival was never precise. My father would spend only a month with us and leave us there until the end of summer. It had been two years since our last visit so there was a great joy about going back.

But which was home, really? Our allegiance was hopelessly divided. We loved our stay in the small village in the French mountains, the fragrance of the fields, the gathering of our extended family, the comforting sounds of their lilting southern voices. But after summer's end, when it was time to return to our white-washed Moroccan villa shaded by the big eucalyptus tree, its rooms cool and dark, our immediate family reacquainting ourselves with the exotic surroundings, the move felt right. I was at home; my space was my own.

Paternal attention became somewhat diluted once my brother was back, and in a way I welcomed the respite. Climbing trees and similar activities had lost their appeal. I was growing up. My mother had given me a small brooch on my ninth birthday, a pretty ceramic rose that I treasured for a long time. Retreating often to my own room, gaily decorated with a flowery fabric, I read away. I discovered *David Copperfield* (in French), which I read and reread for many years afterwards. His misfortunes touched me to the core. I decided then I would become a writer. Lying on the bed, pencil in hand, I started my first story in a brand new lined notebook. I did not realize until later that my first sentences were very similar to Dickens'—only the names were changed. After a full page of writing, I became discouraged and decided to abandon my efforts. It was my last attempt in those days to become an author.

Fall was coming, and it was decided I would return to the lycée. Again I accepted the decision with equanimity. I had missed only half a year of school, so catching up would not be too hard. Not only that, but we would be moving at the end of the school year to another house, a brand new one being built farther out in the country, with a view on a small valley and plenty of room to roam around. Life was changing fast and Villa Blanche would soon become part of the past.

# HOMEWORK

## 1934-1936

∾

Only a loving but stern father could make us tremble. Death, in those days, had no power over us. As youngsters we grew up in its shadow, watching the living and the dead go by the backyard of our new house, the chanting bearers carrying corpses on frail litters to their final resting place. Funerals from the impoverished village that stretched over the next hill were a near daily occurrence.

But if death had no power, boredom did. Now that Jacques and I were both being tutored at home, we had few playmates, and time weighed heavily since the seasons in Morocco hardly changed. Any distraction from our books was welcome, and so as soon as we heard the funeral chants, very faint at first, from far back in the hills, we'd run to a good but discreet vantage point in back of our house from which we could see over the wall.

First we would catch a distant glimpse of the

mourners, following a bend in the fields. Then they would disappear into a small gully, to reemerge on the wide dirt path skirting our yard. Though they all praised Allah, we could tell from the dirges whether a man or a woman lay under the white shroud.

Many a time a newborn lay at the woman's side. But it was always an all male procession, with four bearers carrying the litter, one of them chanting a refrain and the other three responding in unison with the rest of the mourners. Back at the village, we knew, the women would be wailing and screaming in the prescribed way. We had seen them a few times, erupting from their houses without their veils, discarding even their headscarves with yells and imprecations, scratching at their cheeks, and then holding onto the litter in a futile but well choreographed attempt to retain the newly deceased. Hired female mourners brought extra honor to the family that could afford them, their cheeks showing the streaks of countless scratches, thus sparing the faces of the bereaved womenfolk.

Outside the house of the deceased, the usually hot sun would have prevented any lengthy scene, however, and soon the cortege would be on its way. Death had been declared only a few hours earlier, with a piece of hot ember placed on the thumb as proof. Aware that our presence was barely tolerated on one side and frowned upon on the other by the older members of our household, still we could not help but be attracted by the scene, shivering a little at the procession going by as we imagined the body with the burnt thumb under the tight white shroud.

The cemetery was not far away, sprawled over undulant fields that like our fairly isolated house lay well outside the ancient city's fortified walls. Facing east toward Mecca, unmarked white-limed mounds were set helter-skelter among weeds and wildflowers, taking over the sides of the dirt road and the adjoining fields. During breaks from schoolwork, we often traipsed through the grounds as we did all our surroundings, looking for human bones or skulls that might have surfaced after a strong rain. We never found any, as we did not dare each other to look that hard. But there was a limit to our thrill seeking. When we came across families sitting on tombs, talking to their dead or sharing a meal, we retreated in silence.


Eventually, a typhus epidemic put an end to our graveyard wanderings. When vans started pulling up one bright afternoon and lined up row after row of shrouded bodies for burial, we lost all predilection for the white-studded field.

But it was only sometime later, when we witnessed among a crowd of taunting village children the long, solitary agony of a starving mule abandoned by the roadside, its legs kicking circular grooves in the sand, that we finally comprehended the awesomeness of it all.

∽

# LA CONDITION DES FEMMES

## 1938

It was a strange noise, like a cat meowing. The feeble cry startled me, but I did not slow down to investigate. I couldn't, I was so late already. In my mind I kept seeing the anxious face of my mother peering out the window, watching for my return. At this very moment she was probably reproaching herself for having sent me on an errand in the native town so late in the day. Dusk was falling fast.

But why should she worry? I could take care of myself. In any case, I was now safely out the gates of the Arab quarter and halfway through the vacant field, the undulating no-man's-land that separated the old town from the newer European settlement. The path through the high weeds was an easy shortcut, well known to me, thus spelling no danger. But the cry was disturbing. I wondered how many unwanted litters had been thrown behind the thorny bushes here and left to die.

Walking quickly, I looked through the foliage for any stirring. There was none. The weeds around me suddenly took on a hostile look as the December sun slid behind the ancient walls of the town at my back, their shadows covering my path. Ahead, the higher ground remained lit, the lush colors of the green vegetation and red clay dirt made more vivid by the oblique rays of the sun.

Again I heard the noise, and then I saw them coming toward me: a woman followed by a man, both half running down the path. I quickly moved out of the way to let them pass. I knew at once that the noises came from her. One hand to her face, she was crying as silently as she could, but despair was never so obvious. Her stifled sobs had a weak yet high pitch, like those of a young animal in pain. I looked away, not wanting to intrude on a private sorrow. But as I did I was struck by her beauty, which no tears could mar. Her face was flawless, though very pale, as if it never saw the sun.

Lowering my eyes, I saw her bare feet, white and delicate, emerging, as she ran, from under the hem of a long gown, the kind one imagines women kept at home would wear in the security of enclosed walls. It was not an Arab dress, suggesting a world unfamiliar to me. Long-sleeved, gathered at the waist, with a bit of lace high around the neck, it had the flavor of times gone by, with its dainty flowered pattern in light cotton, very chaste attire indeed.

It was cold, mind you. Running and stumbling down the red clay path, she had no shawl, no wrap against the early winter weather. Her heavy mane of black hair, loosely tied, flapped behind her. Right on her heels was a small, repulsive-looking older man, a head shorter at least, wearing a nondescript *djellabah* and the black cap of a Moroccan Jew. As he ran he kept waving his arms, and as they passed I saw that with every step he was silently hitting her in the back of the neck. They were heading straight toward the *mellah*, the Jewish quarter of the old town. Husband, father, who owned her?

Probably the former. Fathers did not usually beat marriageable daughters about the head. I must be witnessing the return of an unfaithful or abused wife, grabbed coatless from whatever refuge she had found outside the old quarter. In his silent and systematic violence the man's fury was palpable. Instinct told me not to intervene and add to his rage. Why should she bear the brunt of my outraged feelings? I suspected the ordeal was not over for her, and that the worst would come behind the privacy of their own walls.

So they went on their way and I on mine, sharing her silent sobbing. At the age of fifteen, it was my first real lesson on *la condition des femmes.*

# ZOHRA IN THE MORNING

❧

Mornings came heralded by the loud braying of donkeys. Roosters, far and near, would answer. Dawn then emerged very fast over the bare hills to the east. Every day during the warm season, the bright summer sun rose quickly to dissipate the freshness of the night. For months, not one cloud marred the sky. A vague hum of wakening rose from all over the land. Soon Zohra would emerge from the small half-hidden hamlet a short distance from where we lived, walking slowly down to the vacant field abutting the side of our walled garden.

Below the field and in back of our property was a large dirt trail linking a populous settlement beyond the eastern hills to Rabat, west of us, its ancient red walls stretching over the small valley. The far side of the trail across from our garden was bordered by cacti that served as a barrier for well-tended vineyards beyond that sloped down the gentle valley to the river. Men and women, some leading donkeys carrying heavy loads of turnips and watermelons, slowly and steadily headed to town, exchanging formal greetings in passing, endless inquiries about health and relatives and customary praises for the Almighty, without any change of pace in their progress.

The spot in the middle of the field held an attraction for Zohra, making her way down from the higher ground of the hamlet soon after dawn. Tall and slender, walking slowly, she carried on her head a silver teapot, and under it, her two slippers resting on the scarf under which she wrapped her hair with a knot at the back. No Arab woman, except for the wrong kind, dared show her hair, and Zorah's was well hidden, pulled tight under the knot.

She would proceed in a regal way, her head straight, her shoulders back, as if she knew she was beautiful. She always wore a long tunic of coarse white cotton, turned grey from usage. Bound at her waist with a red braided cord, it fell to her ankles. Unlike her neighbors who, despite the heat, swaddled themselves in layers and layers of clothing, she wore nothing else: that was very evident. The folds of the tunic over her breasts and hips made her look like a Greek statue come to life.

Every morning, seemingly unmindful of the stream of people down on the trail and the casual stares from our household, she selected an open place in the field, usually a small dirt bank. Laying her slippers aside, her teapot in one hand, she would sit down and start pouring a little water over her feet. She rubbed them gently. This was a long, slow, loving task. Taking the bottom of her tunic, she would wipe her feet and slide them into the leather slippers. Then she crouched down on her heels, resting awhile in a position she seemed to find very comfortable. It was time to tend to her face. With a little more water from the spout of the teapot on her hands now clean and smooth from rubbing, she dabbed her eyes, then her cheeks. Some of the water would run down to her elbows, where she would catch it, patting dry the inside of her forearms. In a final gesture, she pressed her hennaed hands together, her long fingers curved outward, until they dried. The few drops of water left in the pot were then scattered on the thirsty soil. Quickly she would rearrange her scarf over her hair, replace the teapot carefully on top of her head, and, without any visible effort, straighten up, stretch out to her full height, and walk away. Her ablutions were over.

Not too many women could afford such abandon and carefree ways. Usually only men went out in the open, either to meditate or tend to their needs. But you gathered that her conduct was somehow tolerated by her neighbors. As a woman, she had little value. She was known to be barren, and worse, she was severely pock-marked. It was a shock to discover this the first time you came close to her. You could not tell whether she might have been pretty or not. The pocks had wiped away whatever meaning a face can have. Yet her eyes, dark and shiny, showed assurance and disdain.

Not being first-choice material for marriage, it was

not surprising that she had been given in wedlock to a small, scraggly-bearded, lisping older man with a poorly stocked vegetable shop. Despite her barrenness, she must have contented him. Out to buy a pound or two of potatoes or a few green peppers, you would wait, time and again, in front of the open shop calling his name. Finally he would emerge through the curtains separating their room from the stall. You could hear her strong, impudent laugh in the back. Swiftly weighing the staples, he would cock an ear, trying to catch what she was saying. Yes, indeed, he seemed a happy man.

*Going on sixteen, Meknes, 1940*

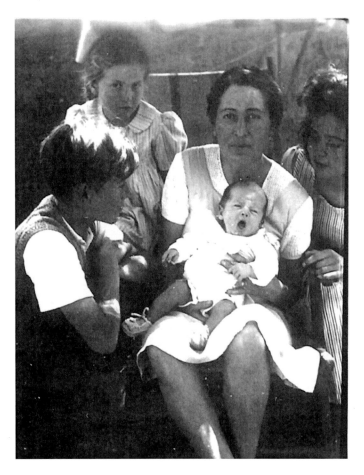

*Maman with new baby, 1940*

*Ancient royal stables, Meknes*

*Fantasia, Meknes*

*Vegetable seller in Medina*

*Stream in Ifrane*

# FLIGHTS, PART ONE

Summer 1937 – Spring 1938

∽

Ifrane was the ultimate escape from our daily lives on the Moroccan coast. When first told by our parents that we would be taking a three-week trip to the Atlas Mountains—the name evoking tremendous power for me—we had visions of green meadows at the bottom of a valley, of a glittering stream cutting through them and mountains in the background. We were ecstatic. It would be like being in France again. Otherwise we would have had to stay home through a boring summer vacation, living mostly indoors because of the heat. While we did have the seashore for cooling off, according to our mother, it was too much of a hassle: first a bus to catch, then a rowboat across the river in order to reach the beach. In spite of our begging, such outings had become rare. Thus, we were delighted at the prospect of a trip to this new place.

As is to be expected, reality hardly ever matches one's dream. Ifrane would not be as we'd imagined. Still, in time we grew to love the place, not only for itself, but also for what happened there during our adolescence. It was a special kind of love, always mixed with some uneasiness from the odd encounters that came along the way. I use the collective "we" since my brother Jacques was my constant companion, and although his recollection of those days may have differed from mine at times, it was pretty much our shared memory.

The morning we left Rabat for the mountains, we boarded a bus with our mother before the sun came up. Our father would drive up a few days later in the family car. The bus was one of those lumbering vehicles always filled to capacity with Moroccans and Westerners, its rooftop overflowing with more passengers and bundles of all sizes, including our luggage, tied up beside a bunch of chickens. It was still dark when we left home, and as our bus drove out of the city I remember a vivid dawn over the bare red earth of the fields, the sun's rays filtering through the eucalyptus trees bordering the road. There was very little traffic this early. Occasionally, after much honking from our driver, we would pass a donkey, his rider sitting on its back end, prodding his mount with hanging feet. We whizzed by a few camels padding along on the soft dirt by the road behind a single shepherd. At thirteen, I was eager to take it all in. I could have still been at home in bed, missing all that excitement!

After stops at two bustling marketplaces in the middle of flat, empty land and exchanges of merchandise and passengers, the bus drove on, crossing a few gullies before skirting terraced slopes filled with almond trees in neat rows. The red earth had changed to grey. Soon, the road took us through the rolling vineyards, orchards, and well-tended fields that surrounded Meknes, where we would change buses. Again we honked our way through the crowded gates of the gray-walled medina, then across a final ravine to reach the newer, European town. Before coming to a stop, we made out in the distant mist the wall-like silhouette of the Atlas Mountains.

In Meknes, most of the Arab passengers left our company, and my younger siblings elbowed their way to window seats on the cleaner and less crowded bus that awaited us. Soon after we left the town, the landscape flattened into grayish-brown fields sprinkled with a few farm compounds sheltered by trees. A pack of big dogs appeared, running in the open, and somebody pointed out to us that they were jackals.

Soon the bus was grinding gears as it started to climb a sharp embankment, an opening between two cliffs. We went up and up until we reached a small settlement at the top. Rocky and treeless, that first plateau of the Atlas Mountains already had a different flavor from the plains. When we got off to stretch our legs, the air, though hot, felt brisk and dry. The few people milling around were dressed differently, among them unveiled women wearing multicolored blankets on their backs, instead of the all white traditional *heik* worn in the coastal towns, with simple scarves hiding their hair. We were in Berber country.

We were promised that the last leg of our trip would be short, welcome news as we were getting tired. At first the lunar landscape of craggy rocks along the road did not appear too welcoming. Small hills with scrubby vegetation appeared on both sides. Painfully the bus lumbered on up the side of a steep incline, honking at every curve. Around one turn, we finally caught a glimpse down below of a mountain stream cascading under lush vegetation. We saw it and then we didn't.

All of a sudden, around a turn, a house loomed over the road on top of a cliff. Unlike the usual flat-roofed Moroccan homes, it had a sloping red tile roof and a terrace overlooking the ravine; at the next turn another one appeared, and another. By now, the bus had reached an open area scattered with more rocks and rather incongruous Swiss-looking chalets of different colors. A few small hotels became visible in the background. We made a right turn by the main street and, after a block, drove into the big bare shed of the bus terminal. We were in Ifrane! Our luggage was handed down and the rest of the passengers quickly disappeared. We were left by ourselves, lightheaded from the change in altitude, trying to regain our bearings.

We started out on foot looking for the small chalet that had been reserved for us in that strange place. Soon the main street dissolved into a gravel road that seemed to lead nowhere. Then we noticed two

Moroccan riders on horseback in flowing white robes, big muskets slung across their backs and whips in their hands, two *Moghaznis,* as they were called, the local police. In between them was the sad sight of about twenty men in black and white striped uniforms dragging chains. They were walking away from mounds of crushed stones of different sizes on the side of the unfinished road and would not look at us. We had gone beyond the limit of Ifrane into a land of unsuspected brutality.

We turned around as quickly as we could. As we did, I touched my face and, to my horror, saw my hand was full of blood. It was just a nosebleed, probably brought on by the altitude, but in my memory it would always be tied to the sight of those prisoners. My mother produced a handkerchief to stem the flow, while somebody appeared from out of nowhere to rescue our bedraggled family and guide us to our assigned chalet. It turned out to be a rather primitive and Spartan lodging. On our first day, Ifrane had turned out to be a big disappointment indeed.

But the bright clear bracing morning that greeted us the next day changed our mood. We could not wait to explore the small new village and the green meadow below, which had recently been landscaped as a park with trees along the stream that ran through it. From narrow wooden bridges, we stared down into clear ponds beside the stream, mesmerized by the sight of winged insects treading on the surface. We discovered small falls whose noise delighted us. In our North African life, the murmur of running water in a stream was a rare thing to hear. A swimming pool fed by part of the stream in the middle of the park won the day, along with a small café with a vine-covered patio that welcomed us with cool lemonade. When our father came to join us for the weekend with the family car, we were able to discover trails into the woody hills dwarfed by huge cedar trees over mossy rocks where big bunches of wild peonies grew undisturbed. We went mushroom hunting and picked morels and found violets by the stream.

By the time we had to return home to the muggy summer of our coastal town, we had grown quite fond of the place. We had no way of knowing then that Ifrane was going to be much more than a summer escape in our lives.


A year later, Papa, thinking about changing careers, decided to take a leave of absence in order to prepare for exams qualifying him for a new position in Paris. Since we were homeschooled, he decided the best way for all of us to study would be to return to Ifrane early in the springtime and stay about four months. Exciting news for us: anything to escape the boredom of stay-at-home schooling was a great prospect. Having no schoolmates, we had no friends to miss. Again we would rent a chalet, away from the comforts of home. It took time to persuade my mother, but Papa was very persuasive. Finally we packed up and went.

Springtime in the Atlas Mountains can be quite overcast and miserable or quite beautiful and enjoyable, but there was one constant: the very cold nights. We found that out early on, as we spent our evenings huddled around a central wood stove under a meager light. But if the sun shone in the morning, we would roll a carpet and blankets into the car and find a new spot up in the hills under the cedar trees or down at a clearing along the stream. Being a small summer resort, the village was almost deserted, with only a few hardy Europeans staying on throughout the year. We would meet at the post office or the general store or the restaurant where we ordered takeout food. The local Berbers were even scarcer.

Lying on a blanket under a tree with a book under my chin as the sun quickly warmed the land was a most enjoyable feeling. I managed to study in spite of all the distractions. It was a dizzying experience, the feel of the earth under me, with myriad tiny creatures around, the daisies and violets by the stream, the dank mushroom smells... His back against a tree, my father would study, with an occasional glance at us, while my brother, fidgety as always, looked for an escape from his assigned work. I'd find that quite annoying, but then he would be the one to discover new things around us, a different insect or a new flower or a secret path, and often I would go with him to explore. Together, turning up stones, we discovered whitish and very lethargic scorpions hiding under them; we would poke them, waiting for a reaction, before moving on.

Under the cedars, I learned to translate Virgil, and the surroundings rendered his verses very poetic to me.

As I see it now, I broke a sound barrier then: I started reading an English novel without having to translate it into French in my head, a revelation. I also became acquainted with algebra in the unlikely setting of the small path along the stream. It was a chilly and humid morning, just perfect for picking morels. We did that too, but for my benefit Papa used a stick to draw some new symbols in the dirt, showed how letters could replace numbers and that infinity was greater than a philosophical concept. I was just becoming aware that math was a discipline in which he was proficient. I had not seen a textbook in years.

I was naturally drawn by the French Romantic period, Chateaubriand, Hugo, Vigny, and was prone to tears when reading them aloud. Distractions from studying were all around us but at the same time became part of our education. After a few hours immersed in a book or a discussion, we picnicked or followed wild trails leading nowhere. Two young scientists, friends of friends of my parents, would sometimes join us for a walk in the woods and uncovered for us another world of small creatures hardly visible to the naked eye. Some evenings were spent at their place, a lonely house upstream set up as a lab, smelling of formaldehyde. Sent by the Academy of Science in Paris, they were studying aquatic creatures in the region. Newly married and to my eyes very much in love, they brought much-needed gaiety into our lives. The notion that scientists could have a sense of humor was novel to me. Traipsing along on their scientific excursions was another benefit of our unorthodox education.

Early one afternoon as we roamed the woods together with me lagging behind, I sensed a big shadowy presence right above me in the trees. It was frightening: I ran to my companions just as the shadow disappeared. They walked back, combed the woods, and found nothing, not a trace. But I knew some creature had been watching us, and it was agreed it must have been a Barbary ape. Although we knew they were around, it had never entered our thoughts that we might encounter one. To be watched from above by unseen eyes was a little disturbing, reminding us that this was after all North Africa.

As the second month passed, exploring the cedar forest lost something of its appeal, but at the same time we became increasingly aware of the creatures living there. We learned to recognize the fresh traces of wild boars hunting for mushrooms, some so recent that we knew they were very close, and we stayed on our guard.

When the weather warmed up, we stayed close to the cool area along the stream, bringing our lunch along with our books. We still had complete solitude since the summer people had not arrived yet. One day while reading quietly with just the sound of water trickling downstream, we were startled by the noise of breaking branches and the snorting of a horse. In the clearing there suddenly appeared a man on horseback dressed in flowing robes, musket in hand. As we stood up in surprise, he greeted us in Arabic. My father answered him in kind, and he told us he was looking for an escaped prisoner. Had we seen him, or anything else suspicious? Of course we had not, and we shook our heads.

Nodding courteously to us, he disappeared in an instant. But still we heard distant noises, voices and dogs barking. All along, I was hoping the man they were hunting would get away. At the village, we had heard that often prisoners would escape to go back to their tribes to finish important business, like getting even with their accusers, and then return to the prison and surrender themselves. The practice was more or less a *caida* (custom), and fairly well accepted in that part of the country.

Within the confines of the resort, we had few contacts with the Berbers save for those helping at the hotels or the chalets. We did have a glimpse of the cramped settlement of small shops with shiny tin roofs that had sprouted in a barren gully along with the construction of the new resort. Wandering through it once, we were met with an odd mixture of curiosity and indifference. We were aware that just beyond the forest lay the small prison camp, but we never saw it. Arab justice was different from our own and it was understood that we had to accept the way it was meted out.

Thus, in this near idyllic setting, save for that dark undercurrent, we were nearing the end of our stay, anticipating our return home and our projected summer trip to France. It was the spring of 1938; I was not yet fourteen.

But dark clouds were gathering on the horizon. Every day, my father waited eagerly for the newspaper that came in the afternoon on the only bus reaching the village. I would go with him to the general store to fetch it, along with fresh bread and his cigarettes. There, along with the owner and a few other customers, we gathered around a crackling radio for news of the world. Eagerly I listened to the conversation that followed. One day I heard them talking around the counter about which cities had been bombed in the civil war in Spain, and about the concept of "open cities," safe zones, and how agreements could be respected...

For the first time, I realized they were speaking about the threat of war gathering strength throughout Europe. I tried to understand the growing unease of the adults around us. War to me was a thing of the past, a historic event from way before I was born that would never happen again. My father was too preoccupied preparing for his exams and tutoring us for me to ask many questions. Then it was time to leave Ifrane. The prospect of going to France for a summer stay after a three-year absence now filled our thoughts. We would get ready for the trip as soon as we got back to the comfort of our house in Rabat.

Three years would pass before we saw Ifrane again. By the time we returned from our family visit to France in late August of 1938, the drums of war had become louder. That summer, the Germans had invaded part of

Czechoslovakia, and the Allies made peace in Munich.

A year later, war was declared.

# TRAIN RIDE TO MEKNES

## 1939 - 1940

❧

The gendarmes knocked on our door in August on the second day of hostilities and gave our father orders to report to his unit the next morning. Living in French North Africa, we were far from any immediate zone of conflict, but from the start our lives changed. That very afternoon after the gendarmes' visit, we piled into our small Renault and made a run to the French part of town for staples. Rabat, normally staid and quiet outside its medina, had its main street filled that day with animated people reading aloud pro- clamations on posters along the arcades. Strangers were talking to strangers, discussing the event and reminiscing about the last Great War, the one so destructive it was described as the war to end all wars. That earlier time, so present in many people's shared memory, was to me ancient history, irrelevant until now. I had just turned fifteen.

The next morning at the train station, I was in tears,

the younger ones in a daze, as we said goodbye to our father. Since he was the only driver in the family, we had all walked the two miles to the station in the early dawn to arrive on time. In the station, my mother had to console and reason with me: although he was a sergeant in the infantry, my father was in the reserves and would probably not be shipped out to the front in France. His assignment was, after all, to help guard the only dam in Morocco. But we were at war…

After a last quick hug and final reminders to us all about this and that, Papa boarded the waiting train bursting with colonial troops in uniforms of various kinds, many Senegalese with deep tribal scars on their cheeks, all of them hanging out of windows and filling the back platforms of the cars, all in high spirits, yelling and singing. It was an intimidating sight. But right behind our father, a middle-aged civilian with a knapsack on his back jumped onto the train, holding a fishing pole. That made us feel somewhat better. At least they were both heading toward the same place. The train was already moving away. In seconds, it disappeared under the station. We walked back, slowly, to a very empty house, exchanging few words.


Chemical warfare was feared. Within weeks, makeshift gas masks made of cotton had been distributed as a stopgap measure with the promise that real ones would be provided later. Police roamed the neighborhoods enforcing blackout regulations. Absolutely no light was to be seen from the outside.

Shutterless windows had to be painted black.

Little by little, a certain malaise replaced the excitement of feeling ourselves a country at war. Most of the men in the French population had been called up, and there seemed to be a subtly different mood among the Arabs, a slight aloofness we had not been aware of before. Living as we did in the country outside the city walls, our sense of vulnerability grew one day when a friend of my father's, a career army officer, came to give us a handgun. My mother would have no part of it. So after showing me how to use it, he left it loaded, and we hid it out of sight of the younger children on the highest bookshelf in the hall. We had been robbed many times in the past, but had never feared harm. A broom handle was all my father kept to ward off intruders. Now it seemed there could be some real danger. I did not quite understand its exact nature, but felt the same kind of insecurity that I had at times when I wandered too far by myself into the maze of the medina.

When the gun was first placed in my hands, I was troubled. I kept reminding myself that it was just to scare intruders and never to be used. Still, I was proud to become the family protector, but being only fifteen I did not lose sleep over it. The gun was there, secure, loaded, and handy. Little by little I forgot its presence.

War stalled in Europe for the next few months and life resumed semi-normalcy without the head of the family. We listened to the same radio communiqués from the European front; each army stayed encamped behind its fortified line. Because of his fluency in several languages, my father had been reassigned to a military censorship center in the hill town of Meknes, headquarters of the French Foreign Legion and home to, among other nationalities, many exiled Germans. Outside the town there was also a regular army base that included among its soldiers *Goums*, fierce Berbers from the Atlas Mountains.

There was joy all around at Christmastime when it was decided that we would all go join our father. He had written of finding us a nice apartment in town in one of those long, affectionate notes the mail brought almost every day for my mother. She would read them aloud to us, except for a few passages, and then she would blush. But his letters also showed concern about our education. By then he had been homeschooling us for several years, and our studies slacked off in his absence. I was preparing for an early attempt at my baccalaureate at the end of the school year, and it never crossed our minds that a war could interrupt such a significant event.

Happy plans for a reunion in Meknes after Christmas were made more meaningful when we learned our mother was expecting again. The day finally came when the house was closed and the gun returned to its owner. This time, a horse-drawn carriage brought us to the railway station. There, we walked down the steps to the open lower platform, bordered along its length by palm trees and carefully tended flowerbeds and with tunnels at both ends. Along the tracks, the same state of confusion reigned as when my father had left us four months earlier. Soldiers, civilians, Arabs,

Westerners, and packages of all shapes and sizes filled every available space. The train was late. At long last we felt faint tremors. Suddenly and loudly, the locomotive emerged from a tunnel, briefly seeing the light of day before being engulfed again in darkness as it rolled to a stop under the station. The tracks ran underground the whole length of the city.

Just as before, soldiers were hanging out the windows, waving at the crowd. We rushed frantically from one car to another, stumbling over suitcases, trying not to get separated. We finally learned that the space reserved for civilians was at the far end of the train. Still on the platform, holding my six-year-old sister's hand tightly, I took the lead, constantly looking back for my mother and brother who were struggling to keep up with me, while trying to ignore the jeering and shouting of soldiers calling at me to join them.

At the next to last car, we were helped on board, and seconds later the train started to move. We inched our way toward a compartment, where my mother was given a seat. By then our railcar was in the tunnel under the station, gathering speed. Standing in the darkened aisle with my brother and sister, sandwiched between boxes and windows, I watched the yellow dome light flicker above us and took a long breath of relief and happiness. Soon we emerged from the side of the plateau where the city spread into marshes and sped across the bridge over the riverbed into the bright Moroccan daylight.

The elation of leaving soon gave way to lassitude. Still standing in the aisle, I swayed with the car's motion. The monotony of the landscape added to the fatigue in my limbs. The train was following the coastline along a gentle depression that obscured any view of the ocean. All we could see was a reddish flatland intermingled with green fields. It was January, the middle of the fertile and rainy season. Scattered sparsely on the land were clusters of dark, low-slung Bedouin tents amidst grazing sheep. Young shepherds, leaning on their sticks, watched us go by.

We stopped frequently in the middle of nowhere. Soldiers would get off and soldiers would get on, with no visible military installations nearby. My sister kept sliding off the boxes she had climbed on, asking constantly if we had arrived yet. Weariness etched my mother's face as she sat in the corner, wrapped in her maroon wool coat. She kept her eyes on the fidgety girl out in the aisle, trying to calm her down with reassuring but barely audible words.

After one stop, we caught sight of the locomotive as it rounded a curve up ahead. We were leaving the coast, heading inland toward the hills. It was getting cold in the unheated train, although the sun was at its peak. Soon, like a snake, the convoy entered a small valley. On either side were well-tended terraced fields. Rows of almond trees filled the lower steps. The red land of the coast had changed to a grayish soil. Very slowly the train climbed to a plateau: again a flattened-out terrain, broken only once by a deep gorge, arid and rocky. We had just a tantalizing glance, through the trestles whipping by our windows, of a small stream among the stones below before the landscape leveled off again.

Meknes could not be too far now. Over four hours had passed since we'd left Rabat: we were hungry and thirsty. Knowing the trip was coming to an end, the three of us sat with resignation on suitcases cluttering the aisle until a man standing at the window drew our attention. We followed his glance. Stretched out in a pinkish mist, the Atlas Mountains loomed toward the east in an unbroken line, like a wall.

Suddenly the train veered to one side, skirting a slight hill. Crowning it was a long, grey medieval-looking turreted wall containing a dense city. Unlike our own town of Rabat, all white with red ochre ramparts, here the town's grey rooftops reflected the color of its walls, its skyline broken by the single, straight steeples of its many mosques. Veering away from the medina, the train crawled at a snail's pace up another hill toward the French settlement, smaller but more spacious with its gardens and wider streets, and then came to a halt.

My father was waiting in the crowd. In spite of his uniform we recognized him immediately and rushed into his arms. My mother followed. Perhaps because of the unfamiliar circumstance of our reunion, he looked somber. After gathering our suitcases, we walked a few steps together and then stopped when we heard the train moving. We watched it leave. In seconds, the tracks were empty.

"How unkempt you children look!" Papa said.

I touched my long hair; I had twisted it into a bun to look older and it had come undone. I looked at my brother and sister and saw their faces smudged with soot from the train. But why such a solemn face? I wished he looked happier. Yet I was old enough to know that world events weighed heavily on him. Trailing behind him and my mother, we soon reached the center of town. It was animated, soldiers everywhere, café terraces spilling onto crowded sidewalks. Suddenly my father turned his head and took a long and gentle look at us. I smiled. War or no war, we were together again.

Four months later, a new sister would be born there in the military hospital. The very morning of her birth, news from the front would come hard and fast: Germany was invading France. Within a few days, across the sea, the country would be overrun and defeated. My father would be discharged and we would go back home to Rabat, not knowing what was to happen next. But on Armistice Day in June 1940, I sat for my exams.

❧

# FLIGHTS, PART TWO

*August* 1941, *April* 1942

❧

Three years had passed since our last visit to Ifrane. Although since then our family had welcomed a new child, another little girl, those years had been bleak, separated as we were from our family in France and with the news from Europe going from bad to worse. We had scant knowledge of our relatives' whereabouts. France was now under the authority of a Vichy government, and so too was its protectorate, Morocco.

Yet to our delight, when the summer of 1941 came, we three older children learned we would be allowed to go on our own to spend two weeks in Ifrane to escape the heat, mosquitoes, and parental anxiety. This time we would stay at a family friend's small hotel, nominally under their supervision since my sister was only ten, although I would really be in charge.

It was heaven to be heading again to the place where we had enjoyed such freedom. We rode in the same lumbering bus we had taken years earlier, to the same terminal. But when we arrived, we found the resort much livelier than before. As soon as we had unpacked at the hotel, we went downstairs and immediately met young people our age. Later in the day, swimming in the pool by the stream, we met a few more from other towns, and older people from varied and mysterious backgrounds. Like us, many were staying in small hotels or cottages, while others lived in a makeshift camp outside the village. We met them again in the only outdoor café in the village. The flirting ways, the casual ease and nonchalance shown by our new friends, appealed to us right away, and nearly a week passed as we three savored our carefree days, with no time for family squabbles.

Then one night, toward dawn, we were awakened from a sound sleep by noises in the hallway outside our room, heavy footsteps and loud voices saying *"Nein, nein!"* and then hearty laughter. Were Germans around?

But there was no sign of any new arrivals in the morning. The day promised to be beautiful, and we went swimming in the pool before joining our new friends at the roller skating rink by the small café. It was while we were skating that we caught sight of those dreaded uniforms for the first time.

Although it was known that Germans were around Morocco as part of the Armistice Commission based in Casablanca, exacting goods and food supplies for Germany, until that morning we had never seen any. The officers, about eight of them, strolled onto the terrace, grabbed the front tables that had miraculously opened up, and ordered drinks from the bevy of waiters hovering around them. Two of them, dark-haired with young, handsome faces, removed their hats, laying them carefully on the next table. Beside the casual dress of the summer people, the trappings of their uniforms, the black insignias on their caps and lapels, the shiny black boots stretched out with abandon under the bright sun, made them stand out like birds of ill omen. We caught the harsh foreign sounds of their voices as they bantered with one another, watching us.

It felt strange to be skating under their eyes. One of the better skaters in our group detached herself from the rest and took off around the rink, her arms swaying wildly, to finish in a long arabesque, aiming her foot in the air at the new arrivals in a mocking gesture as she turned.

"Please, Mado," someone said as she rejoined us at the far end of the rink, "please, behave yourself. Don't look for trouble." She shrugged her shoulders as if she did not care. Some of the youngest, like my sister, tried to keep on skating, but the rest of us were already unhooking the clamps of our skates.

The waiters were still rushing back and forth to the sprawled group in uniform. The officers had loosened the tops of their tunics and, despite the heat, looked very much at ease as they talked and laughed. They seemed in great spirits. Whiffs of the feared tongue floated to the far end of the rink, a true assault on Gallic ears.

As we left to go our separate ways, we agreed to meet that evening in the campground. The sight of the new arrivals at the café was troubling to us, and we needed the reassurance of being together again. We had no illusions about the precariousness of daily life for some of those among us. Still, our group had jelled in a casual and lighthearted way within a few days of meeting at the pool. The usual reserve of the fully dressed had dissolved quickly by the water's edge. Many of us had exchanged our full names and hometowns, but others had offered none and no one would have thought of asking: too much knowledge in those days could be dangerous. Nicknames were found, provocative and funny, leading to mild flirtations. Escaping for a short while the closed and rigid society of the protectorate, we felt the exhilaration of being with contemporaries who asked nothing of us. Often when we gathered, the disapproval of our elders was obvious. Their sidelong glances said it all: what spoiled, frivolous youth in times like these! And now, unexpectedly, the Germans had appeared in our midst, reinforcing the alienation we felt from the world around us.

Eager to join the others at the campsite, my brother and I sneaked out of the hotel that night, leaving our sister sound asleep. In the moonlight, we headed toward the sharp outline of the scattered tents and big rocks that marked the confines of the camp. A cold breeze was blowing from the desert, encircling the mountain range, but the stones still felt warm to the touch. We took a seat among our friends and watched the last glowing embers of a dying campfire. After a few songs and some small talk, we became silent, absorbed in private thoughts. Beyond one of the rocks, someone was still strumming a guitar. When he finished, someone finally piped up from the shadows: "What are the Krauts doing here?"

No one answered. The guitar player began an Armenian ballad about homesickness in a foreign land. In the night air, his voice sounded beautiful, the song incredibly sad. The moon rose, casting strange shadows around the rocks and stunted trees. One of the girls suddenly stood up. "Please stop! I can't bear it anymore." The musician complied.

In the general silence that followed, a small voice piped up: "What about a picnic tomorrow?"

The suggestion was met with a chorus of approval. Plans were eagerly made to go downstream to a small but spectacular waterfall. Since food was rationed, we would share whatever we could scrounge from our hotels and secret hoards, and as always there would be bread, fruit, and wine. After agreeing to meet near the pool just before noon, we broke up and tramped back to our lodgings in the chilly night.

The usual bright sunshine greeted us the next day as we three met our friends in the meadow below the pool, piling our bags and backpacks on the ground. Our spirits had recovered fully. While waiting for late-comers, my brother and two or three others went to pick buttercups and daisies, which they braided into crowns. Just above the small meadow, beyond twisted oaks, the cedar forest sheltered mossy rocks and beds of wild and pungent peonies. With a leap or two, the small raiding party brought down armfuls of the pink and purple flowers, so that when the signal came to proceed down the narrow path along the stream, nearly everyone sported a crown of flowers or a single droopy blossom over the ear.

The pleasant surroundings, perhaps commonplace in other countries, were almost unimaginable in this part of Africa, yet the place existed, natural and benign, made to be enjoyed. Here, within sight of the walkers, pale violets and morels grew in the damp humus by the stream. Going single file or in couples down the path toward the falls, we could not escape the feeling that the spot existed like a persistent dream, so well hidden was it on the high plateau.

We were all there: Mado, the red-haired girl, and Maddy, the blonde, the only ones whose real names were used; then Soprano, Big Feet, Argentina, the Dutch Broad, the Lieutenant (apparently on furlough), Curly (me), the Armenian, my siblings of course, and so on—it was a spirited group. Prospects for a picnic are always a joyous affair, but this one had a touch of unreality that made it all the more pleasant. Going down the path, we yodeled and sang, looking like a bunch of mad Ophelias. In rare moments of silence, we heard the soft gurgling of the stream.

Soon a low rumbling, faint at first, then building up to a thunderous din, announced the falls. Appearing suddenly under an arch of trees, the stream waters, softly rounded at the top, fell spreading like a curtain into a billowing mist, finally settling, calm and limpid, into a shallow basin before continuing on their course.

The bright flowers were discarded and gear dropped as several stripped to their bathing suits and splashed happily in the shallow pool, yelling at each other over the roaring noise. Flexing his muscles, suave Argentina, probably the oldest of the group since he sported a mustache, stood briefly on a flat stone just under the falls and, looking up, started to climb. Staggering under the weight of the water, he hugged the rock, feeling for crevices. He half disappeared under the frosted shield of the falling water. Then slowly, very slowly, he re-emerged, hoisting himself up at one top corner of the falls, capturing everyone's attention. Two others ventured the climb but, stunned by the mass of water, had to give up. Argentina savored his victory.

The falls were found to be too noisy for the picnic and a spot above them was selected near a mulberry tree whose gnarled limbs hid the banks of the stream. While bottles were uncorked and readily sampled, a cloth was spread out in the clearing and bags of food set in the fork of tree where it split into several branches. Long loaves of bread sticking out of their bags were propped in the tree's fork up against the trunk, safe from ground ants and the like. Some drowsy and harmless scorpions were discovered under a few small stones and carefully removed. We were famished! Settling around the cloth, most of us started exchanging food while the others still indulged in mild horseplay.

Then it happened. I saw one of the girls, I believe it

was Maddy, lift a tin cup to her lips and stop in midair, the cup never reaching her mouth, her eyes round with astonishment. She did not utter a sound, but only pointed at the tree. A few of us turned our heads in that direction, while the others, unaware, kept eating and laughing. Maddy's companion, the one we called the Lieutenant, jumped to his feet.

Out of nowhere, a thin yellowish hand followed by a disembodied bony arm was crawling down the bark of the tree until the long fingers touched, then grabbed one of the loaves. For a second we were speechless, just pointing at the tree, and then we shouted in disbelief. The Lieutenant and two other fellows rushed behind the tree into the underbrush by the water's edge. Amid the noise of breaking branches, we heard a violent scuffle, followed by the bark of a bloodhound coming from another direction.

Looking grim and purposeful, the Lieutenant reappeared, holding his catch in front of him, twisting the man's long arms behind him so that his shoulders stuck out and his head slumped. In his torn clothes, he looked old and exhausted.

At that instant, a dog emerged from the trees and lunged at the man. Halfway in the air, it somersaulted, held back by a chain. Two Arab horsemen appeared in flowing garb with muskets slung on their backs. In seconds, while one dragged the howling dog aside, the other quickly dismounted and slapped manacles on the man's wrists, still held by the Lieutenant, and then locked them to a chain attached to the horse. No words were spoken to the prisoner as he stood there, resigned, casting only a longing look at the food on the ground. I grabbed some food for him, as did others, but the guard pushed the offerings aside. With brief thanks in Arabic to our group and a salute to the Lieutenant, who responded in kind, the guard jumped on his mount and proceeded up the narrow path by which we had come, his barefoot prisoner in tow. His companion took up the rear, keeping his own chained creature in check. Almost instantly they disappeared, as if the whole episode had never happened.

Except for the loaf of bread that now lay untouched on the ground, the setting had hardly been disturbed by the brief appearance of these strangers in our midst. Had a few minutes been removed from our collective memory, the picnic would have continued its lighthearted course—but obviously they could not be. We sat down on the ground and resumed sharing food, chastened by what had just happened. My sister snuggled close to me.

"Did you see that hand creeping down the tree?" Maddy said to no one in particular. The Lieutenant seemed subdued. Although he had received his share of thanks from about everyone, he looked as if he had expected more. We were indeed grateful, but the joyous spell we all felt earlier walking down to the falls had dissipated. The capture had been so brutal and swift that we felt the fragility of our new bonds.

We did not linger after eating. Soon, of common accord, signals were exchanged to pack up and return to the village, this time by a different way. We avoided the path we had taken earlier, now the route for the horsemen and their quarry.

We forded the stream quietly. The way back to the village on the other side proved more difficult because of the underbrush. We could hear intermittent noises of traffic from the paved road somewhere ahead. Emerging from a small wooded area, we saw the road just above us, carved into the rocky slope. Holding hands, we helped one another up the steep embankment and jumped over the guardrail onto the narrow road just in time to catch the roar of motors coming around the bend. We ran to safety on the other side as two German military command cars went past us at full speed. I had a fleeting glimpse of their ramrod-straight occupants before they disappeared around another bend toward the village. Ah, they loved the place also...

As soon as we reached the village, we went our separate ways with the promise to meet again soon, but I had my doubts. I knew then that Ifrane would always be a temporary escape, a place to which you went for comfort and security, but also a place to flee.

On reaching our hotel, we were told we had to leave the next morning. More German officers had arrived and two were demanding our room. So we packed, and with little time for goodbyes, we took the old bus home early the next day.

Big news awaited us on our return. It had been decided in our absence that my brother and I would return to school in the fall, about a month away. I suspected parental fatigue lay behind the decision. But what!!! Back to school?! We had not been in one for years! A scary feeling: how did one conduct oneself in a classroom? My studies so far had consisted mostly of reading and then discussing what I had covered. Now I would have to listen to someone lecturing a class and learn to take notes. Still, my brother and I did not put up an argument. Indeed, despite our trepidation, we secretly welcomed the news. After Ifrane, we were now ready for contemporaries.

So, after more than six years' absence, I went back to school to prepare for my second baccalaureate, slowly renewing acquaintance with my classmates from years before. It took time to understand their interactions, their language, and the classroom routine. A few shy Moroccan girls were now in the class and I felt a strong kinship with them. I passed a lot of time daydreaming.

For Morocco, it was a cold winter that year. In our free time, we knitted sweaters and scarves for our countrymen imprisoned in Germany. The news from the Eastern Front was dire: the Germans were consolidating their hold on Europe, and only glowing German communiqués were dispersed in our flimsy one-page paper. Listening to the London BBC radio could get you in real trouble. People started spying on each other, neighbors on neighbors, and my father's government job was jeopardized because he wouldn't wear a *Francisque*, symbol of allegiance to Maréchal Pétain. The lapel decoration was not obligatory, but wearing it certainly helped to maintain one's good standing.

That winter, too, news came from Ifrane about the

sudden and brutal death of Mado, the most daring of our group there, a death unrelated to the war. It made the news in the Casablanca papers: "Horrible skiing accident in the mountains! Girl ripped open by rocks underlying the snow." The report was followed by an editorial about the folly of skiing in the Atlas Mountains. Other news filtered in: two of the young men in our group had been caught in a surveillance net and were being held in camps for *indésirables*, probably lacking identity papers. Another of our former companions stirred our imagination by stealing a boat and escaping German detection to join the British in Gibraltar. That did not make the papers. The police jailed a girl I knew for suspected Gaullist activities. That was not in the papers either.

During the winter, the Germans' presence in Morocco slowly dissipated as they left for more pressing duties elsewhere. Rumor had it that many were being called to the Eastern Front in Poland and the Balkans. In time, they would have to endure miseries of their own. Meanwhile I still wondered, whatever happened to the fellow we called Argentina?


The school year was passing so far without a hitch. I had become used to the routine but shared my class-mates' apprehension of the final exams that would so strongly impact our lives, determining whether we could pursue our studies or not. The pressure was on.

So when Easter vacation came around, I was grateful that we would be allowed, Jacques and I, to go back once more to Ifrane, where the family friend was getting her hotel ready for the summer season.

The weather was still chilly and the place pretty empty, but at sixteen and seventeen, we loved that feeling of freedom from family, from rules at home, from chores, from old habits, and now from school. Going to different schools in the daytime, we would now have a few days simply to enjoy each other's company.

As usual, my brother found unique ways of amusing himself, and I often went along. Again we roamed the forest, lay on the warm rocks in the clearings, and picked armfuls of spring flowers to bring back to the hotel. Once, as we were quibbling over which way to go, we encountered a family of apes climbing the trunk of a huge cedar tree. Two females with babies on their back stared down at us, baring their teeth and grunting. We stopped in our tracks and in a second they disappeared into the treetops. We quickly ran out of the woods before a big male could come on the scene, as apes were known to throw stones and hurt people when disturbed. A priest bicycling to the village had even been killed.

Some of our best times were in the evening. A handful of the usual year-round residents from the village would gather and play bridge by the hotel parlor stove while we played checkers and listened to the small talk. It felt very comfortable. We loved to listen to the old-timers' stories. They joked about who would be the lucky fourth to join the three persons lying in the new non-Moslem cemetery, probably waiting for another hand of bridge.

In addition to the old-timers, three others were regular visitors at the bridge table. We found these men great company: funny, whimsical, and very British. They were curious about us, a pair of adolescents, and we were certainly curious about them. We were told they were businessmen from Casablanca being kept under surveillance by the Vichy Government. England being at war with Germany, they were considered suspicious and had been sent away to Ifrane. Around the country, internment camps had been set up for people with dubious nationalities, to comply with the terms of the Armistice. The three may not have been trusted in a camp as those were too close to the main towns. At any rate, here in Ifrane, they were in *résidence surveillée*, a kind of house arrest.

And sure enough, every night we were there, the gendarmes came to check on them while they played bridge with our friend the hotel owner and others. Their interactions with the police were always amiable, and after the card playing, tea and talk would follow. They seemed to take their light internment with a great sense of humor. Here in the middle of nowhere, from their assigned quarters at another small hotel nearby, they always arrived dressed up in coats and ties, with a peony or spray of violets in their *boutonnières*. For us, that was class… I thought one of them looked especially dashing.

On the last morning of our vacation, having said a special goodbye to our three English friends the night before and taken a solemn pledge to meet again in ten years at the same place, my brother and I went one more time deep into the cedar forest for a final look. We discovered a lovely clearing we had not chanced on before, fairly free of rocks and brush and quite open on one side. Wary of apes or wild boars hunting for mushrooms, I begged my brother to turn back. As we were about to retrace our steps, my fears came true as we heard strange noises coming from the woods behind us. Not now, not on our last day!

But they turned out to be human voices. We could not believe our eyes as three men emerged in the clearing, our British friends, who seemed as surprised as we were to meet there. How had they escaped police surveillance, we wondered, since they were not supposed to go beyond the village confines? We greeted them but did not linger as they did not seem at all eager to make small talk. After a final wave, we quickly left.

The encounter marked the end of our final escape to Ifrane. A day later it was back to school and exams, and sad news at home. From German-occupied Paris, a terse telegram finally reached us: our grandmother had died two months earlier. We also learned that our scientist friends, being Jewish, were in hiding somewhere in southern France. Hitler was spreading his conquest toward Russia…

But a surprise awaited me as I came home from school one afternoon shortly after returning from Ifrane, news from my mother's friend at the hotel. Our British acquaintances had suddenly disappeared, vanished! A small biplane had been seen in the area and must have scooped them up from a small clearing in the forest a short time later. We applauded the news as we remembered the setting and how close we had come to derailing their plans.

Five months later the tide turned in the war, with the Allies landing in North Africa. Shortly after, we received word that one of them, the dashing one, was enquiring about us and our well-being. He turned out to be at the head of the British Intelligence Service in the area and had flown back to London with his companions to help the Allied Army with preparations for the landing. Some two years later, with the war still on, he found out about my engagement to an American serviceman. I was touched when he sent word that he would help with any red tape if need be. Then we lost track, but I always wondered what became of him.

The solemn promise that we would all meet again in Ifrane never materialized, of course. Still, when the tenth year came around, I thought back on our pact and silently acknowledged it. Our friends were probably scattered around the world, as I was; I just hoped that no harm had befallen them before peace finally came.

Here I was, a young housewife and mother transplanted from Morocco to the American Midwest, but as I remembered our promise, Ifrane once again regained the mythic dimensions of my youth.

# AGAINST THE CLOCK

## Spring 1942

✍

Imagine that the year is 1942, a very cruel year in Europe. Imagine it is springtime in a North African town. Much less cruel here, but the semblance of normalcy barely hides the precariousness of everyday life, the absence of most young men—some of them war prisoners in Germany, others having joined the free French in Dakar—the sudden disappearance of others, the rumors for lack of news, the snitches everywhere, the time-consuming search for food because of the Allied blockade, all this under a balmy and enervating sun lulling one to old habits anchored from the days before the occurrence of what people refer to simply as *"les évenements,"* the events.

"There was a phone call, a long distance phone call from Casablanca...," said the man to his wife late that afternoon when he came home from his office. She put down her knitting as he looked at her in the strange, beseeching way she knew foretold bad news. They had no phone in the house, which was just as well since all private lines were tapped. She looked at him, not saying a word, waiting to hear more, as their sixteen-year-old daughter came into the living room.

"It was Marcel." He paused, and then went on: "He could not say too much on the phone. Remember the young woman he brought over several weeks ago? Well..." He turned aside, not wanting to face his daughter. "Well, she killed herself. Marcel did not add much more, only that she got tired of running, gave up and cut her wrists open—a horrible mess!

"Please, please, don't ask me any more because that's all I know, that's all I can tell you."

He quickly turned around to avoid any questions and left for the solitude of their bedroom, closing the door behind him. A pall fell over the house.

The girl stood transfixed as she watched her mother wail: "Why would she do such a thing? How awful... It doesn't make any sense. Even if she was in some kind of trouble, she was finally safe here, safer here in Morocco than anywhere else. She must have had some friends... What was she running from?"

The mother kept on sobbing, and the rest of the children gathered awkwardly and silently around her. Everyone in the household remembered the visit that had taken place some three weeks earlier. Now, with the tragic news, an aura of inevitability would surround the memory forever.

❧

Nothing had really taken place that day, just a short and very civil interruption in the household routine. But that one small break in their routine had made the visit difficult to forget.

Think back, just think back: It's almost time for the noon meal, the most important part of the day for a French family. They are about to gather around the table, no small undertaking since the four children range in age from toddler to teenagers.

The father is on his way from the office, on lunch break. Since the war has deprived him of his car, he is running up and down the back dirt roads that will take him to the family villa in the hills outside the city. He is rather proud of his physical stamina, of the way he can still sprint like the soccer player he used to be. Usually one of the younger children watches for him by the garden gate, waiting to be carried into the house on his shoulders for a grand entrance. But time is short: the clock is ticking for all to get back to work, back to school.

On the landing outside the kitchen door, an Arab maid is crouching over a small three-legged clay stove, stirring over hot embers a vegetable stew made of eggplant, rutabagas, and tomatoes. If it's a lucky day, a few pieces of mutton will have been added. The kitchen is nearly useless now since there is no more gas and electricity is sporadic. Even water is scarce. But the smell of the *tagine* is rather nice due to the herbs simmering in the stew. Potatoes are no more and pasta is scarce, so the *tagine* will be eaten with some dark bread made from wheat and chaff. It is a monotonous meal. Luckily, as always, there are oranges for dessert.

The table has been set by the older daughter in the dining room, one of her regular tasks. Meanwhile the mother is scurrying around, looking rather hassled at this busy time of day, calling the various children to the dinner table while dashing to the bathroom for one last quick look at the mirror and a fast dab of lipstick. She has spent most of the morning scouring the markets for staples. "Come on, children, go wash your hands! Papa is home, let's eat. He's got to get back to the office."

The busy, tedious, but unnerving routine of the midday meal, when schoolwork is discussed and maternal complaints are aired, is about to start. The family is converging on the dining room when the doorbell rings.

Who on earth could be coming at this time? Peddlers usually amble through the back courtyard and crouch patiently by the kitchen door until someone comes around. No, it was definitely the front door bell, and everybody scampers into the kitchen until the caller leaves and they can eat. The teenage son is sent out to the front hall to open the door.

At the sounds of recognition and friendly exclamations, Papa goes into the front hall to meet the caller, his youngest in tow hanging on to his pant legs. "Hey!" he yells back to his wife, who is back in the kitchen muttering about the bad timing. "It's Marcel! What a nice surprise! It's been quite a while... What are you doing in town?" He calls back again, "Come, Simone, it's Marcel!"

Marcel had a nonchalant way of appearing and

disappearing in their lives. Chance had abruptly thrown the two men together in a Moroccan military outpost at the onset of the war two years earlier, and nearly as fast thrown them out when France was so suddenly defeated. A young fellow in his mid-twenties, with rather distinctive features, an artsy dilettante who enchanted the children with nonsensical bits of poetry, Marcel made light of his personal predicament. Being a Jew, he was much safer in Morocco, but his well-known family was being hounded in Europe, although neither he nor anybody else understood at the time the true extent of their plight. But he knew he could count on the older man for help when needed. After their mutual discharge from the army, his friend had hired him, a German-born French national, to tutor the children in their language lessons, helping him survive many lean days. He then found him a fairly safe job in Casablanca, which is why they rarely see him anymore.

Warmly shaking Marcel's hand, the father motions him into the hall and then notices that his friend is not alone. Behind him stands a woman, a rather pretty blonde who looks a little older than the youthful Marcel. Introductions are made and greetings exchanged, and he ushers the visitors into the parlor. He calls to his wife, "Simone, Simone, we have visitors!"

Busy untying her apron and checking her hair, Simone dashes out from the kitchen to the outdoors stove to mind the stew.

"Not yet, not yet," she tells the maid who is waiting to serve, then corrals the children in the hallway. "Be patient and we'll eat soon," she cautions them. After rubbing her hands on her hips to gain some composure, she makes her entrance in the parlor. She greets Marcel warmly as he introduces his companion, and offers her hand to the young woman. A good hostess, she excuses herself and soon returns with a tray of small glasses of port wine. Toasts are in order.

But after Marcel's usual inquiries about the children and their progress, the conversation lags. A clock ticks in the background. Such an ill-timed visit… The rather well-dressed woman has a definite accent. She could be Polish. Quiet and perhaps intimidated, she lets Marcel talk, but even he seems unusually subdued. They came by bus for the day from Casablanca, he explains; she is the friend of an acquaintance of his and has just arrived in the country after many months of traveling. The talk remains full of discreet French civility. One does not ask probing questions, war or no war.

The clock's ticking seems to grow louder. Kitchen smells pervade the room. Marcel and his companion finally get up and take their leave.


Closing the door behind them, the man asks his wife: "Should we have invited them for lunch?"

She looks at him in dismay. "We don't have enough food for today. I came back from the market with hardly anything."

"You could make a salad," he begs of her. "I'm sure you can find something in the kitchen to serve."

She quickly relents, saying somewhat reproach-fully: "I was actually waiting for you to ask them. Is it too late?"

He rushes to the front door and opens it in time to see the couple walking away on the small dirt road toward the bus stop by the highway. Collaring his teenage son, he tells him to run after them. "Please ask them to come back and have lunch with us."

While his wife hurries to the kitchen to supervise the changed menu, he stands by the front door, hoping the boy will reach them before they disappear around the slight curve in the road. He does. The man sees his friend turn around to listen to the boy, and sees him shake his head. The gesture says it all: No, but thanks anyway.

Slowly his son comes back to him... Soon a lumbering bus will take them back to an indifferent town while the family eats a very silent meal.

After the tragic news of the young woman's death, the image of these two on the road going back to their respective fates would take hold in the collective family memory. Was the lack of simple generosity toward a complete stranger the final indignity that pushed her over the brink? They could not even remember her name. But that final image, of the two on the road, persisted in their minds for the rest of their lives.

And Marcel? He kept in touch for a while. He made out all right, it seems. When the war ended, his scattered family regrouped and got him to return to

France. He continued his carefree ways; at least that was the impression he gave his friends when they saw him in Paris years later. He never mentioned the blond woman, and neither did they.

# BEYOND THE WALLS

September 1942

∾

*"Le ciel pardessus le toit, si bleu, si calme..."*

Soaking wet, I lie still in my hospital bed so that the searing pain does not flare anew. Only my fingers inch toward my bandaged abdomen for reassurance that the ordeal is over, the incision neatly stitched, the troublesome appendix out for good. My first year of college will be starting soon and I have to be ready! Nailed to the bed by a level of suffering I've never experienced before, I make an effort to float out of my body toward the open window.

It is wartime, and although the fighting is far away, Morocco is under blockade. The only working hospital in the area is a quiet compound of old colonial military pavilions by the ocean's edge. Overseen by a ghostly Mother Superior in white garb, the hospital provides only the barest essential care from military doctors. An aspirin parsimoniously given is all that I am allowed for pain. So I try to leave the physical me to its ordeal, while a peaceful feeling wraps itself around the one that can get away, wafting lightly over the bed and melting with the scant sights and sounds of the world outside. They start to penetrate as if I had no skin and make the pain almost pleasurable. Bits of melody come and go...

Can it be late afternoon? Just another hot and humid day, like always in early fall near the ocean. No breeze, no relief will be coming from the water's edge. The faint noises seem suspended in the air, clear and slow: a man calling another man, a bit of song started and abandoned, a yell, all have a crystalline quality tempered at times by the muted sounds of ocean surf, a stronger wave perhaps hitting the rocks with more than usual force.

The long, narrow window reveals a patch of intense blue sky crowded into a corner by part of a rooftop. Several sparrows are balancing on the wire strung across the eaves, constantly changing spaces. That is all I can see. A faint aroma of smoke signals the lighting of fires outside for the evening meal in the army camp beyond the hospital grounds. I remember that the day before, while waiting for surgery, I had heard the endless drilling of new recruits. But all is calm now. Verlaine's verses come to mind:

*Le ciel est pardessus le toit*
*Si bleu, si calme.*
*Un arbre pardessus le toit*
*Berce sa palme…*

The sky is over the rooftop
So blue, so calm.
A tree over the rooftop
Gently sways…

Poor Verlaine, watching life unfold through a cell window after squandering his own! I had sung those very words earlier in the summer, trying out a ballad on the piano. Now I am living them!

A moan comes out of my throat, catching me unawares. The pain makes me toss on my pillow, and I notice I am not alone. A young nun is watching by the bedside before taking my pulse. Then she lifts tangled and wet strands of hair away from my face and smiles.

"I'm sorry, Sister," I manage to say. "I did not mean to startle you."

Her fingers feel cool to the touch. She really does not look too much older than me.

"Close your eyes and try to relax," she replies. "It would be good if you could fall asleep."

With small muffled steps, she retreats to the corner of the room, her face hidden by her coif and veil. Still as a statue, she too is looking through the open window. Can she see the ocean? Maybe, if the outside walls are not too high. For sure, she must have a view of the grounds, with their white and green pavilions set amidst the palm trees. I would like to ask her: "What can you see, Sister?"

But she is so quiet I do not want to intrude. I use the silence to take stock of my surroundings, an enormous room all in white. My narrow metal bed covered in chipped white paint is the main piece of furniture; next to it is an equally weathered nightstand. One straight-back chair stands guard near the bed, and in the corner of the room is a big white marble fireplace. I am smothered by all the whiteness, which mingles with the pain. I want to turn away and look toward the window again.

But then I discover the flowers. They must have been there all the time, high up on the mantelpiece: big, beautiful pink and yellow roses. The nun walks toward them now. She fingers the vase, rearranges the stems, her face close to the opened blooms.

"Your mother brought them while you were still in surgery," she says. "How lovely, lovely!"

She breathes in their scent. Just then, Mother Superior comes in and, without looking at me, stares down her charge, who now hangs her head in submission, her hands hidden in the fold of her surplice. A nod from the older woman dismisses her and she disappears into the silent hall. The smell of roses has not reached me, but the sight of them is all the comfort I need.

I am the next object of scrutiny for Mother Superior. Without a word, sheets are pulled off, the bandage exposed. I look at the bright red stain seeping through. How big is the scar? Mother Superior is poking my abdomen with light cool hands. Her silver crucifix is dangling over my nose. I cry out:

"Why must it hurt so much?"

She straightens up and looks at me. "There is hardly any pain that one cannot bear. Remember that patience is a Christian virtue and soon your body will heal…"

I have the feeling that the body is one of her lesser concerns. I see myself as I must appear to her, a rather pampered girl. I start to close my eyes to escape the forbidding presence. But she brings to my lips an aluminum cup of tepid water.

"Drink a bit, please, very slowly." She is not about to be ignored.

She continues: "I believe somebody came to see you earlier this afternoon, soon after they brought you back from surgery. A young man… He slipped in while our backs were turned. Visitors are not allowed so soon, except of course your immediate family."

She says no more, and finally I am alone again. I seem to remember now. Back through the haze of awakening, I can just recall the visit, an anxious face, a hand reaching for mine, a wet cotton swab on my parched lips. When I opened my eyes again, he was gone. A scary sight I must have been! There is a small mirror on the nightstand, but I dare not reach for it.

Beyond the window, the sky has paled. The sparrows along the wire are getting feisty, arguing loudly, flitting around. All of a sudden they are gone. The windows should be closed soon, as the ocean fog will be rolling in at any time, along with an army of mosquitoes...

The pain has not let up much. A long night is approaching and I am dreading it.

*Patience, patience. Yes, I know, Mother Superior... When you come in, I'll close my eyes and I will not complain. I will not. Don't patience and suffering go together? Aren't they the same? An old Latin word comes to mind. "Pati": I am suffering, I endure.*

*All right, Mother, I'll be patient.* But there is so much happening outside these walls and I can't wait!

# THE DAY NOTHING HAPPENED

## November 1942

~

Nothing had really happened since that fateful Sunday morning three days earlier when all hell had broken loose just as the family was getting ready to go on a picnic in the woods.

They had planned it for a long time, finally gathering enough bicycles for every member except the youngest, who would travel behind her mother in a small wicker seat. The picnic baskets were half full, and they were finishing breakfast. The day promised to be beautiful: a clear, warm North African autumn day. But distant muffled sounds had been heard earlier, as if the ocean surf were pounding the rough coastline with more than usual strength. That seemed strange, since the sun shone brightly and the air was calm.

Suddenly from out of nowhere an awful noise was upon them. The second child, a slight boy of about sixteen, rushed to the window just as two low-flying planes with strange markings swooped over the rooftop, their machine guns clearly visible, spewing fireworks all around in the midst of deafening explosions.

It was all over in a few seconds. Everything became dreadfully silent. Then the family rushed at one another, wondering what had happened. They realized at once that the youngest had disappeared. They had begun a panicked search for her in all the rooms when some motion under a bed attracted their attention. A neighborhood German shepherd had unaccountably found its way there, and hanging onto its neck was the toddler. In spite of soothing words, the two refused to move and stayed under the bed, clinging to each other. They had to be dragged out and pulled apart, then herded quickly into the cellar with the rest of the household.

The group was joined by an old Arab woman who, passing on the road, had somehow climbed over the gate when the planes attacked. Sitting on her haunches, she prayed continuously to her saints.

But soon time began to hang heavy down there. Nothing to do but sit on some old planks and a cobwebby trunk wondering aloud about those planes: where had they come from? After a while, the children were hungry, and the oldest went back upstairs to retrieve the picnic baskets from the kitchen. The planes had not returned. Everyone waited a little longer and then, after some hesitation, went back upstairs, their ears acutely attuned for any unusual sound.

Clearly the area had been shelled. The small Rabat

airfield nearby might have been the target, but for whom? Although the airfield was under German control, there were no German troops around, just Vichy authorities at the small Air Force headquarters within the compound.

Could it be the Americans? Had they finally crossed the ocean, and were they landing on the beaches? That would mean the muffled sounds heard earlier were not from an angry sea, but from the naval guns at the base in Casablanca some fifty miles away. The long-awaited event, could it really be happening at last?

The radio was turned on, but there was no news except for a short announcement that the country had been attacked by unnamed forces and that the invaders were being repulsed. Martial music blared, followed by Arabic singing, nasal and discordant. Impossible to get the BBC in London, the airwaves were jammed. The children watched quietly as their parents paced the living room, voicing their concerns: The situation was insane. Would the few French forces stationed along the coast fight the Americans on orders from Vichy? The Germans had insured that the French had hardly any troops or arms. With luck, any such resistance should be over quickly.

Later that afternoon, as they peered out through their windows at the road that lay beyond the vineyard bordering the garden, they saw people streaming in the direction of the city, their belongings tied to the handlebars of bicycles. The proximity of the airfield must have frightened them.

But where could one go, and how? Their car had been immobilized for nearly three years, propped grotesquely on cement blocks, its tires confiscated at the beginning of the war, when the French army was readying itself to fight the Germans and needed rubber. So the family waited, standing by the radio. Newspaper circulation had been temporarily discontinued. In between broadcasts of terse military communiqués in which the invaders were finally acknowledged as an American landing force, they heard announcements that all schools and banks were being closed and stiff curfews imposed.

For a sixteen-year-old boy, this was heady news. Finally there'd be some excitement and action in this dull place!

Yet the next day dragged on, desperately long, with nothing to do but wait. Toward noon, planes appeared to the north over the horizon and then turned around. Heavy smoke billowed far away. Were they bombing the small harbor in Port Lyautey? The boy climbed up -onto the flat roof of the house and, in the distance, saw the planes dive in formation and then puffs of smoke appear on the ground. But no noise reached his ears. To him, it appeared like a strange ballet without any music. Suddenly they were gone. A few round black clouds rose slowly on the horizon.

Two more days passed. Since most stores had closed, food supplies were low. The boy's mother sent him to town on his bicycle to look for any grocery stores that might be open. There, in the half-deserted city, he stopped to watch a small detachment of men in colorful colonial uniforms marching in step, turning north toward the river. A few hecklers were yelling insults in their wake, and others pleaded with them to turn around: "Please do not fight the Americans!"

But they had orders and they were going out to battle. They soon disappeared from view, still in step, their faces taut and impassive. On the curb, a woman was crying at the sight of them marching off.

The boy returned home empty-handed. The news of the men marching out of town appalled the household. After a meager lunch with the family, he was told to catch up on his homework. He couldn't concentrate, though. When would the Americans come? Where was the fighting?

Life in the household had gone back to a near routine. It was siesta time: the younger children were napping; the parents, apprehensive, were in the garden, under the wisteria, discussing what options they had for the days ahead. Leaving his room, the boy sauntered through the empty kitchen and out to the backyard. He discovered that his bicycle, propped against the house, now had a flat tire. He swore through his teeth, and then thought of his older sister's bike, kept in a small room in back of the garage. Quietly he rolled it outside, tiptoeing on the noisy gravel driveway, and out onto the road. At last, he was on his own.

Pedaling quickly over the deserted roads, he soon reached the avenue running along the ancient red wall encircling the city. Where the wall veered down toward the river, it had crumbled away, revealing the wide vista of the flat, meandering riverbed below. His feet resting on the low frame of the girl's bicycle, his blond hair flying back and his eyes half-closed against the gusty breeze on the slope, he went down the road at break-neck speed.

At the bottom, he made the sharp corner onto the deserted highway paralleling the river. By then he had almost no control over the bicycle, its handlebars shaking in his grip. He was elated. In no time he was approaching the bridge spanning the pungent salt marshes of the riverbed.

He found an eerie scene. The sentries who had guarded the steel girders since the beginning of the war were nowhere to be seen, and he had no problem getting to the other side. There was not a soul around, no traffic, no noise except the wind at his ears.

Beyond the bridge, the road was shaded by stately eucalyptus trees. He kept going at a brisk pace, riding along the smooth area near the center line. It was then that he heard a few indistinct sounds, but he could not guess their origin. As he kept on pedaling, the bursts of noise became stronger and flashes of red came into his field of vision. He realized he was not alone anymore and braked.

Red and khaki, these were the same uniforms he had seen earlier in town. Soldiers appeared by the trees that aligned the road, doing a strange dance around them. Here they were, then they were gone, hidden from view behind the wide tree trunks. What on earth were they doing?

Then he saw the planes just over the treetops, one following another. Their undercarriage skimming the branches, they roared overhead in a fury of flares and explosions. At that very moment, someone with officer's stripes on his sleeves sprang out from behind him and screamed:

"Good God, kid, get the hell out of here!"

As he quickly dismounted to turn around, he noticed a wet spot at his feet surrounding a soft, whitish ball. It looked like a huge, pale raw egg splattered on the pavement. It dawned on him that it was a human brain. He ran, still holding onto the bicycle, toward the nearest tree. The planes disappeared.

Fleeing the scene like an unwelcome intruder, he pedaled frantically toward home. The ride back over the bridge seemed an eternity, and the only noise he heard was the beating of his heart. His legs gave way as he made it to the other side and started up the steep and arduous incline toward town. He got off the bicycle and pushed it until he reached the plateau.

It was suppertime when he finally crept into the house, exhausted. They were already sitting down at the dinner table, except for his father, still coaxing the radio for any kind of news. Swiftly he took his usual place between his sisters. His mother looked at him. "Jacques, where on earth have you been? Have you washed your hands?" She shook her head. "You know, we nearly started without you."

❧

# HEY, MAN, THERE'S A WAR GOING ON...

## Winter 1942-1943

You'll never believe me if I tell you how it started, not in a million years. Here's that rosy-cheeked kid fresh from the States, a replacement for the Chippewa that was so homesick he got catatonic or something— couldn't get anything out of the guy. Just stayed in the tent, on his cot, wouldn't move, wouldn't talk, wouldn't eat. Hell, there's a war going on and we're halfway there. I thought they were kidding when they told us on the ship we were landing in North Africa...

Africa? How come? Where are the Huns? But then, where are the Africans? All we see is just a bunch of Arabs yelling and waving their arms, always wanting to sell us something, and then a few Frenchies, and they don't say much either... Well, anyway, the fun hasn't started yet, we're halfway to the front and this guy is already blotto, can't get anything out of him. Had to ship him home, back to the reservation. Hope for his sake he wasn't faking, or I'll be sure to get my hands on him when I get back.

At least the new guy is wide awake, wants to help, asks questions—boy, does he ask questions! The other fellas in the company have it up to here with his questions, he's getting under their skins. "Don't you ever shut up, kid?" I says. "Yes, Sarge," he says. "Sorry, Sarge." But he keeps going.

Then one day we hear we may be moving on. Could be the real thing—high time we make a move and see some action, and the sooner the better. Let's get it over with so we can pack up for good and go home. Anyway, I'm getting sick and tired of this place, with the thieving natives sneaking in the tents as soon as you turn your back and swiping everything in sight, and then, those uppity French—most of them won't give you the time of day. Kind of hard keeping the men busy while there's nothing to do. So, hell, I'll be glad when we get out of here.

Well, that one day, we get a few passes. Last chance for these, probably. I'm due for one and so is the new kid. I decided why not give him a good time after all. THAT'S MISTAKE NUMBER ONE!

I found out he'd never been with a woman before, never had a good roll in the hay, that sort of stuff. He said he did plenty of necking at drive-ins with girls that wouldn't let him go past first base, 'cause they had principles, they'd say to him. I doubt he even got that far.

"Well, kid," I say to him, "we better remedy that, and the sooner the better. We need a little action here.

Just leave it to me."

He looks at me kind of puzzled.

"Can't vamoose from here without getting a little piece. That's about the only good thing about this godforsaken place."

"OK, Sarge, if you say so," he says.

The men in the company had talked about one establishment just outside town. I'm given a map on an envelope. Can get there by bus or by taxi, no problem. We go by bus. THAT'S MISTAKE NUMBER TWO!

Hell, I'm thinking, there are better ways to spend your money than on taxi fares, with those cutthroat drivers and their broken-down taxis. But they do know the way. Still, the bus's OK, no problem. The guys told us where to get off. The kid is nervous, I can tell. We have to walk out on a gravel road about half a mile through a vacant field. I wouldn't even call it a field: bare red dirt with a few scrubby, prickly bushes. You'd have to be crazy to try and grow anything there. Just beyond a turn is the house, like it says on the map. In fact, it doesn't look any different than any other house, white stucco, flat roof job, smack in the middle of a garden with a wall all around, except it's all by itself in nowhere land. But that's the way they said it'd look, no different. But the girls, oh the girls, choice stuff they said, young ones, dark ones, light ones, they'll treat you like royalty if you show greenbacks and not local money, they said. Have your pick and you won't be sorry. Still, can't see how they could have very many in this one place. But that's what they said...

We get through the gate. The kid trails behind. I

knock on the door. Lo and behold, when it opens, here is this girl, long curly locks down below her shoulders, nice tits showing through a red sweater—yeah, nice. Boy, this one's for me. Tough luck for the kid, he'll have to find his own. I step inside, grab the girl by the waist, bend her backward and kiss her right smack on the lips. Guess I don't count on her screaming. I jump back and a man comes running out, followed by a boy. She goes whimpering to him and he quiets her down. I am downright dumbfounded, if I may say so. They start all that gibbering in French.

"Sorry, oh so sorry," I try to apologize. How to say it to those Frogs? God, I'd like to wring the neck of the guy who gave me the map. The kid is still at my side, looking like an idiot.

The man nods. "No offense." He speaks English!

"Just a mistake, an honest mistake," he says. "I understand. But you did scare my daughter. I think the place you are looking for is further down the hill. It has a neon sign out front." He has a funny smile on his face now. By gory, I think he is enjoying the whole thing. I keep saying: "I'm sorry, truly sorry, didn't mean any harm."

The man says: "That's all right. These are confusing times for everyone." Geesus! All we need is him preaching to us. Naw, I kind of think he's having a little fun. "Please," he says to us, "do sit down for a minute, don't feel bad."

Now I am really confused by Frenchy. So we sit on the living room couch and he talks to the girl who's kind of hiding in the corner near a piano. She shakes her head no. He insists and she shrugs her shoulders. But she comes out slowly and sits down on the piano bench. If you ask me, that's not the type of entertainment I'm after. She starts playing, and she ain't that good, only fair. But that's nice music, like what you hear in church. Wouldn't you know, she hasn't played five minutes before the kid gets up and starts bawling.

"Reminds me of my sister," he says and runs out the front door. 'Course I follow him—I swear that Frenchman got his kicks—what am I sposed to do?

The kid is still bawling up by the road. I'm pissed off. Do I have to play nursemaid to that crybaby? I've got to go visit the girls, come hell or high water. I remember the flask in my jacket, for breaking the ice when the time comes, so to speak. The boys said to watch out for the house vino, it's the pits and you never know what they could slip in it. All right, maybe a little whiskey will do the trick for the kid.

I tell him: "OK, stop the sniveling. Remember, you wear the uniform. Let's have a sip and we'll figure out what to do." So we sit by a ditch along the road and drink a little. Darn if the neon sign ain't flickering beyond another bend down the hill!

"I tell you what," I say to the kid. "Stick around here while I pay a quick visit to the broads, unless you changed your mind."

He says, "No, you go alone, I'll wait here."

"OK," I say, "keep the bottle meanwhile, and I'll be back in a jiff." MISTAKE NUMBER THREE! I shouldn't have taken my eyes off him!

It's nightfall when I get out of the place—we'll have to hustle to make it back to quarters in time. Guess I stayed longer than I meant to, and the vino wasn't that bad either. Feel a little woozy, what the heck...

But there's no kid in sight! Good gawd, what now? What's happened to him? I go up and down the road right back to the bus stop. No, he ain't there. I look in the fields on both sides of the road, 'case he fell asleep in the weeds. I call out his name. No answer. Now it's really dark and my head is splitting. That vino wasn't so good after all. Should've known. Where is the little bastard? I can't show up without him. I'm in charge, remember?

Just when I'm about to call it a day, I hear that squealing and screaming from way beyond the fields. I can see some houses over there, all bunched up. They stand out in the night, they're so white. Never noticed them before. I see shadows moving around and lights flickering, and then, no mistake, there's the kid's voice screaming, "Help, help!"

Can't run too fast. That vino really got to me. I see they're in the middle of the field now, lots of them, all Arabs, men and women in their white gowns, all shouting. The women let loose with these weird, blood-curdling, high-pitched voices that give me the willies. Never heard anything like that before.

Oh, God, I better find Frenchy's house, I say to myself. I stumble through the weeds, past the cathouse. Guess I was crawling when I got to Frenchy's garden wall. I don't remember much how I got there. The place looks closed tight, all shuttered up. They probably can't hear the noise yet. But I see some light. No time to find the gate. Got to admit, I'm pretty soused, couldn't make it over the wall if I tried. So I throw a stone against a shutter: no response. They keep screaming behind me. Can't they hear it in the house? I throw another one. The door opens.

"Ah, you again," says Frenchy, looking real disgusted this time.

"Help! Help!" I say to him, "my buddy's in trouble. They're trying to kill him."

Don't have to say more, he hears it now, that whole damn ruckus they are making. He yells something to people inside the house and, hey, leaps over the wall and runs across the field toward the crowd. I try to follow but can't keep up, legs are spaghetti. By the time I get there, he's in front of the kid, who looks a mess, clothes torn, cap gone. There's enough moonlight to see that much, but I can't tell if he's got blood or mud on his face. My God, those people have stones in their hands and they're about to use them too. The French guy puts his hands out, like *just wait a minute, hold on…* I guess they know him. He must be talking to them in their language, 'cause it sure don't sound French, more like clearing your throat. I don't want them to notice me, so I stay way back in the dark, but I see these two men coming close to him, with raggedy white beards over dark robes. They talk real excited with their hands shaking at the kid and then at their homes. Good Lord, he must have stumbled into one of them. Frenchy starts to smile, like saying *look, he's just drunk, probably meant no harm,* or something like that.

Whatever, it don't go over too well, because the women start their screaming again. Oh my head, you can't believe how they carry on, and now it looks really scary as they all walk closer to Frenchy and the kid. Frenchy don't look too comfortable anymore and the kid seems out of it. They haven't seen me yet and I try to crawl back into the bushes. Damn, what did I get myself into! It could be the end for yours truly...

Just about now, I hear the sweetest sounds I ever dreamed possible, although that seems hard to believe because, to tell the truth, they feel like nails driving into my skull, *vroom, vroom,* motorcycle noises, then siren sounds. Yep, it's the MPs with their white helmets shining in the dark, and a command car right in back. Someone at Frenchy's house must have called for help. Big flashlights shine all over the field, skipping up and down, until they zero in on the screaming natives.

I stumble toward the light. "Help, my buddy there is in trouble!" I think I manage to yell.

I hear the order, "Freeze, soldier!"

Easy for them to say, I can't hardly stand up, but suddenly, like a miracle, I don't hear no screaming anymore, just arguing. Before I know it, I'm sitting in the command car on the backseat next to an MP who don't say nothing, just chews gum. Out in the field, the crowd gets bigger; lots of discussing, arguing, I don't know. Frenchy's right in the middle, probably translating, it takes them forever. Nothing I'd like better than to crawl in the sack back at camp and forget the whole damn day. Well, they come now, two police and between them the kid in handcuffs. They slip 'em on me too.

"What for, guys?" I ask.

"Just tell your story at the station," they say.

When I object, they say: "You're lucky to be alive. Your pal there is accused of rape. They'd like to kill him on the spot. We'd better get the hell out of here before they change their mind."

I can't believe it—he couldn't have! The kid is slumped on the far end of the seat.

"I didn't do nothing, I didn't do nothing," he keeps blubbering. "Couldn't find Sarge and I just knocked on doors and one opened and I fell in."

The MP looks us over, up and down, with a flashlight. Yipes, the kid's face is a mess, blood, snot, and mud. But I must look OK, I think.

Just as we're about to drive off, I see Frenchy running toward us, on the way back to his house. He saved our lives, I suppose. I just don't want to see his face anymore. Makes me feel like an ass, capital A. But he stops and tells the driver:

"No rape, mind you, but he did break into a Moslem house and saw the women without their veils, which is just as bad... I promised he would be punished. So their honor is safe since he was drunk and didn't know what he was doing and will probably forget their faces. Had to quote the Koran to convince them." And he turns around and is gone.

The kid springs from his seat and startles me. He has stopped his sobbing.

"Sarge, believe me. I meant no harm. I got tired of waiting for you and I was sick to my stomach from all that booze. Couldn't find the bus stop. I was just trying to ask for directions."

I believe that, because it's just like him that we nearly got stoned to death on account of him not finding his way home. What's that Koran business all about, I don't rightly know. Frenchy got me there, that's for sure.

But I swear that's the whole story, s'much as I can remember. I'll take the blame for the kid getting us in trouble. But, gee whiz, I better have my head examined next time I feel like doing the kid a favor. Do you know what? All he's worrying now is that his folks will hear about it. Dammit, won't he ever learn anything? Hey, man, there's a war going on.

# THE MAN WHO PAINTED STARS

D o they still remember each other after so many years? The pale, dark-haired Spanish girl, looking old-maidish even in those days, and the thin blond Georgian who swept her off her feet during wartime in North Africa? I hope they do, although the images must now be blurred. Despite the bittersweet end of their story, perhaps their recollection of each other sparks an intensely private and joyous feeling unequaled by what life really intended for them and finally delivered: for her, to be the wife of an older farmworker in Spain and mother of many children; for him, who disappeared without a trace, to drift about in his own country, no doubt. Later on, in America, I saw many who looked just like him hanging around truck stops on old Route 1, from Virginia to Florida. Neither of them could share their memories with others, because who would understand?

Thus the remembrance would stay sweet and unsullied by words, and the once-loved face would become too nebulous to hold for very long, a pleasant memory to recall before sleep finally came. Both bound by a hopeless future, the past, at least, gives them an opening, theirs still, if they have not forgotten each other; some joy that can never be taken from them.

Until I became a part of their love affair, I had known Dolores only slightly, as a shadowy presence in her father's bakery in the Arab hamlet nearby. We had had a nodding acquaintance for years, maintained as such by mutual shyness and her lack of fluency in French and mine in Spanish. She seemed older than me, but her age was difficult to determine. Her frizzy hair and the dry skin crinkling around her restless brown eyes emphasized a long, thin nose in a rather flat face. Seldom heard, the sound of her voice befitted her looks, as her words came out halting and faint.

In the summertime, when school was out, I would often be sent to their house a little before noon and would knock at their front door just as her father and brother were pulling fragrant loaves of all shapes out of the ovens. I used to get a crusty, crown-shaped one in exchange for a few coins. Dressed in drab and loose-fitting clothes, Dolores would hover in the background, her arms and throat demurely covered in spite of the intense heat of the Moroccan sun, a heat that was heightened by the roaring ovens. We would nod at each other, that was all.

Outside their closed-in stucco house, as secretive as those of their Moslem neighbors, there was an old mulberry tree that provided a welcome shade around its exposed roots. Carrying the smell of freshly baked bread from the warm loaf in my hands, I would often pause under the tree to watch the activity surrounding the communal well nearby. A handful of Arab children were usually playing in the powdery dirt, while a few women, their heads carefully wrapped in white scarves, busied themselves around the well. They all wore belted pastel-colored gowns, their long sleeves held back by a soft cord around their shoulders leaving their arms uncovered for daily tasks, their animated chatter almost drowned out by the squeaky sound of the pulley bringing up the small pails of water used to fill the clay amphorae lying on the ground. It was our habit to greet one another in a good-natured way. As soon as I left the shade and darted toward home, I knew they would commiserate about me, so grown up and still unspoken for, just like that Spanish girl withering away under her father's roof.

But a few months after the land was invaded by friendly forces, our lives suddenly changed. For the Arabs in those days, the new arrivals could as well have been moon-men, but the rest of us, accustomed to the slow pace of a warm climate and tempered by the bounds of European etiquette, welcomed the exuberant breed that took over, changing sounds, sights, tempo, and expectations. For the previous three years, war and defeat had cast a shadow over our existence. Now the Americans had arrived, and unlike the other foreigners, welcome or unwelcome, who had come and gone since the war's start, they could not be ignored.

It was clear that these invaders and the boatloads of G.I.s who followed were confused by what they found.

Many seemed to expect bare-breasted women, lush jungles, all that Africa conjured up in those days to an innocent America. Nervous and on their guard at first, somewhat frightening in their strange uniforms, they soon became endearing, sometimes obnoxious, but always quite visible. Their unflagging optimism dissipated the general gloom, and their lively, snappy tunes conquered what was left of the young. Life seemed worth living again, and yet we were merely their first stop on the way to war.

The atmosphere they brought was contagious, and like so many of my contemporaries, I did not escape the attraction. I too fell in love. There was a very brief courtship followed by a very long separation. Still, as I walked to school some months later, I was unprepared for the sight of Dolores strolling arm in arm with a thin blond soldier. She did not seem to notice me.

I hardly would have recognized her had it not been for the plump, dignified mother at her side and the brother trailing behind. Her transfigured face bore no resemblance to the one I knew. Her shiny eyes looked ahead and saw nothing. She had become nearly pretty. A straw hat tamed her hair and she wore an embroidered yellow dress. Dolores?

Her companion helped her gently down the curb, handling her like fragile china. I will never forget the look of adoration she gave him in return.

I saw them together one more time. They were sitting on an old bench near the mulberry tree, his arm around her shoulder. I envied them their time together. Her mother was knitting nearby on the front steps of their house. I can't remember ever seeing Dolores outside again.

We did meet afterwards in the confines of the bakery. As usual, we did not exchange any words, but she smiled at me, although the glow around her had subsided a little. Like all of them passing through, her soldier must have gone on his way in a predawn convoy taking him closer to the European front. There could not have been any goodbyes allowed, there never were. She probably waited one Sunday afternoon for his customary visit, and then the time came when she had to take off her yellow dress, put away that precious pair of silk stockings, and help her mother with the evening meal. She could have had but a faint knowledge of distances, but she must have guessed he was already hundreds of miles away. As for him, from his vantage point in back of an army truck, he was bound to watch helplessly as the road unfolded, each moment widening the space between them.

It was her young brother who came by sometime later, asking me to come and see Dolores. He had started delivering bread on a broken-down bicycle and our house was the first on his rounds. He stammered his request but would not say why she wanted to talk to me. Knowing she would never bring herself to ring our doorbell, I walked over to the bakery that very afternoon, curious but also a little apprehensive. I was well aware that the blond stranger had not been seen for a while and that a lovesick girl was probably grieving quietly behind those austere walls.

I had to knock several times before I heard the

unbolting of the door. Her mother let me in. She smiled in her usual kind manner, then led the way past a darkened room where a strong smell of yeast came from vats along the walls. The ovens on the other side revealed empty racks over faintly glowing embers. Through the doorway ahead, I saw Dolores get up quickly at the sound of our voices.

It was first time I had been in their living quarters. The room, spare and immaculate, held only a table and chairs beside a small corner cupboard. The whitewashed walls were bare except for a hollowed-out stone hanging from a hook. It was an oil lamp, vestige of ancient times, from which a fragile light flickered, perhaps to ward off evil. I was intrigued. But Dolores was greeting me, offering me a chair and thanking me effusively for coming.

"Do you know I am engaged?" she said in that halting and muffled voice of hers, eagerly looking into my face for the surprise her words were bound to bring about. I did not let her down.

"I am so happy for you! Can it be?" My words trailed away as I grabbed her hands. It was the first time we had ever really talked.

"Yes, you saw me with him—it is that American soldier. We are going to marry after the war."

She went to the cupboard and brought out a framed picture, which she handed to me. I studied the face. The features were bland but open. Looking straight into the camera, he wore an unadorned cap set at a rakish angle, his arms folded.

Discreetly, I averted my eyes from the inscription

written in the corner, but saw it anyway: *To Dearest, Darling Dolores from Jim.* The look I had seen on her face that Sunday was here again. As I surrendered the picture, she looked radiant for a moment. Her mother was watching her, basking in the girl's happiness.

How had the two ever met?

Dolores must have guessed my thoughts. "My aunt Juana brought him one day. He got lost in town and nobody could understand him. She can speak a little English, so she talked to him and he followed her to our house."

I could barely catch her heavily accented French. In her excitement she was now talking very fast, the mother nodding in approval and adding her version in Spanish. After so many years of solitude, a flood of words was coming out unchecked. "He came back several times afterwards. Then he told my aunt he wanted to marry me." Dolores paused and blushed slightly, then went on: "He told her he never met anybody like me in America."

Seemingly surprised at her own boldness, she chuckled. A long silence followed, and my imagination filled the gap: the aunt approaching the dour baker and his wife for the family consultation, from which the girl was shut out; the father's grudging acquiescence, then the mother's tears at the thought of separation; and finally, the smile of victory on Aunt Juana's face as she went to join the trembling Dolores in her room.

The courtship itself could not have held much mystery; like mine, it had been too brief. There may have been some handholding under the watchful eyes of the mother, following the timid consent the girl gave to his marriage proposal, witnessed and translated by the eager aunt. A few awkward kisses were no doubt attempted by the young soldier in the rare moments they found themselves alone. But then, the rapture in her eyes would have quickly changed to distress and his lips could only brush her cheeks as her heart pounded away. What could have made her more desirable?

I looked at the plain girl, trying to see her through his eyes. She walked to the table and picked up a small pile of letters. "He has been gone over a month." Her voice again was halting and flat. "These came yesterday." She held up the long envelopes.

Sensing that a request was on her lips, I stalled for time. "Is he with Fifth Army, in Italy perhaps?"

"Ah," she answered, "I am not sure where he is, but he must be far, far away. All I know is that he paints stars."

I had not expected this. "Stars?"

She took my surprise in stride. "Those white stars on those jeeps and trucks, they have to be repainted all the time and that's what he does."

A touch of pride came through her words, and I could not help smiling at the notion of that strange army going to war in such a meticulous way.

She opened one of the envelopes. "You understand English, don't you?"

I nodded.

"I have tried with this," she said, picking a tiny blue booklet off the table, "but I am having trouble."

I had seen the booklet before. Every G.I. had been given one. It dealt with how to ask for directions in French and how to strike up a conversation with local girls.

"Could you please help me with them?" She handed me the letters.

As I started to translate, I felt wrapped in the warmth of her mother's smile. Even after so many years, I still remember how short and formal his first message was. Carefully couched in big printed words, it went something like this:

> *Dearest Doloris*
> *This is to let you know I am fine I hope you*
> *are fine too I will try to rite offen give my*
> *regards to your nice fambly I miss you.*
> > *Love*
> > *Jim*

I sensed from the first words in the next letter that its contents were more passionate and felt some reluctance in going further. I looked up at Dolores. Her eyes had become very bright and intense as she stared at me and waited.

"*Ma très chère Dolores cherie,*" I read aloud. *My dearest darling Doloris*, he had written. His words sounded better than mine, but I persevered.

> *I love you I love you I love you I miss you a*
> *hole lot I want to kiss you and kiss you and*
> *kiss you... I want you in my arms!*

Embarrassment made me glide over my translation. Dolores blushed as she glanced at her mother. Then I stumbled, as the lines became an unreadable and senseless scrawl. Catching a word here and there, I pleaded ignorance and skimmed in confusion through the long, rambling letter. At the very end, though, he wrote clearly that he was sending his paychecks home to Georgia so that they could get married when the war was over, which, of course, was welcome news to all of us.

Together, Dolores and I composed an answer, just as formal and stilted, I fear, as his first letter. I hoped he could read between the lines all the love she had for him. She insisted on signing off, *Your betrothed, Dolores.*

Well, the war in Europe went on and on, for more than two years. Jim did the whole Italian campaign painting stars as Dolores prepared her trousseau. The light from the ancient oil lamp continued to flicker on the wall as we spent many afternoons working on the letters, my schoolbook English improving immensely since I was also writing daily to the young G.I. I was going to marry. When I'd come into the room, Dolores would quickly set her needle aside and place an inkpot and lined paper on the table. She seemed to be always embroidering a bit of decoration around the collar of yet another stiff and demure nightgown.

Eventually the correspondence slowed, or else she managed on her own. I was seldom called anymore.

Peace came and returning warriors claimed their brides. I was one of them. Our wedding was grounds for a neighborhood celebration in the hamlet, and Moroccan pastries were sent to our house. The garden reception had an audience outside the walls comprised of the women and children who usually gathered at the well. But the shutters remained closed at the baker's house. Just a few days earlier, Dolores's mother had sought me out.

"He cannot come back now," she had said. "All the money is gone, his sister in America used it up. She has small children, poor little ones, and she needed that money. He says maybe he'll come later on."

She knew he wouldn't. She also knew it was better this way. She became certain of it when a Spanish widower asked for her daughter's hand a year or two later and took her back to their homeland.

Dolores is an old woman now. Does she remember? Does Jim?

# I WANT YOU TO LOOK AT ME

## 1943

∽

Just as she starts up the wide path along the boulevard leading out of the center of town, the girl becomes conscious of someone staring at her. Having given up on the scarce and broken-down buses going in her direction, resigning herself to the long walk home, as usual she averts her eyes from passers-by, having learned to ignore with seeming indifference the stares, comments, and various gestures often directed at her. It is wartime, after all, and soldiers are swarming in the North African town where she lives, either on their way to the front lines or back for a rest. Many wander about in utter idleness.

But indeed, someone is staring at her. She catches a glimpse of a young man walking in her direction, smiling as he draws closer. Dressed in a French officer's uniform, he goes by slowly, his neck taut and slightly bent to the side, the right sleeve of his tunic turned up at the elbow and secured with a big safety pin.

As she feels his eyes on her, a forgotten scene flashes in her mind: a warm summer afternoon in another town, another setting, some two years earlier. Could this be the same person? She had just turned seventeen then and was heading for the cooler Atlas Mountains, in charge of her two younger siblings. Halfway there in that stopover town, they had waited for a second bus at a nearby sidewalk café. Could this be where she saw him before? It seems like the same face, thinner though, with the same insistent eyes. At the memory, and in case it might be him, she momentarily drops her guard and gives him a quick nod, then looks away. Could it be him?

Shaken by the sight of the flat, empty sleeve, she inhales deeply and hurries on.

She recalls the scene at the café jammed with travelers sitting in the flimsy shade of a few wide umbrellas. Thin slivers of ice were melting fast in the tepid drink she held. Not much older than she, a young man was sitting at the next table with a middle-aged couple. Their eyes met by chance, but he kept on staring at her. She remembers how she blushed and averted her face. The woman at his table, his mother no doubt, was talking in earnest to him. He seemed to answer rather carelessly, looking beyond his own circle, and the girl knew he was still watching her, drawing her into an open complicity while clearly enjoying her confusion.

She cannot forget how, to her surprise, she shared that enjoyment. The warmth she felt spreading from her cheekbones down to her neck was not unpleasant. She had allowed herself to savor the feeling, experiencing a rare and heady sense of freedom, knowing she was just passing through and would soon be gone. Until then, she had thought little of her looks, even despaired of ever attracting anyone. Holding on to the moment, she had turned her eyes on her brother and younger sister sitting beside her, jabbering away in happy anticipation of the cool mountain stream awaiting them.

To her relief, it was soon time to leave. She stood up quickly and followed the younger ones toward the waiting bus, ready for the last part of the journey to the mountains. Under the haze, like a mirage, they were barely visible in the shimmering heat. She could not help but notice, as she walked by, that he was still looking at her. His eyes were peculiar, she thought. Deep blue and unblinking, they had a strange and unsettling effect.

Later on, she would reflect on what had been an auspicious start to the vacation just ahead. But with time, the memory faded, leaving only the special feeling of gratitude one can bestow on perfect strangers that crowds fleeting remembrances. Now, he seems to have surged up again from the past: it could be the same person, and she is troubled by his present state.

Dusk has settled by the time she reaches her house, matching her somber mood. The war in Europe has shifted and all the available young Frenchmen in Morocco have been drafted, including her brother, now eighteen and in training in America to become a pilot.

With little preparation, the majority of young men have been sent to fight in Italy and Southern France. Many have come back wounded; others have not been so lucky. She cannot chase away the vision of that pinned-up empty sleeve on his officer's uniform.

The town is small, and she sees him again and again. Is it just her imagination? It seems that almost every time she goes out on an errand, they cross paths. Again she feels his troubling stare as his lips sketch a soundless greeting; she just nods at him in recognition. Always alone, he never once attempts to speak to her.

What could he be doing all day, that she sees him so often on her way to town? The local hospital is filled with limbless soldiers, and he must be one of them. Is she a coward not to stop and say a few words to him? But the silent stares have gone on too long, and words have become unthinkable.

Increasingly uneasy at the frequency of these encounters, she tries to avoid him. She starts out earlier, she changes her route. But the respite is brief. Soon again, he walks by her with a mocking half-smile as if he has caught her at her game, his unblinking blue eyes not moving from her face. What does he want from her? She convinces herself that he is flaunting the flat, rolled-up sleeve to watch her discomfort: *I am maimed and I want you to look at me.*

She ignores him now. At the faintest sight of his uniform, she rushes by, looking straight ahead, her heart pounding. Obviously the pursuit is on. She dreads going out. She cannot confide her plight to anyone without feeling her fears are vague and childish. She resents the trouble, the guilt he is bringing into her life. Why is he hounding her so?

And then, it stops. At first she is not aware of this. But soon it dawns on her that she has not seen him for a while. She is quietly elated, even laughs at herself for letting him trouble her in that way. How fortunate it is that she has not mentioned him to anybody! What foolishness she has gone through! He is finally part of the past. Trying not to dwell on him, she comes to relish her newfound peace.

Weeks later, crossing the town square one day, she catches a glimpse of the familiar uniform and the slow, barely off-sided gait. She freezes, but the man is walking away. Then it dawns on her: it is the wrong side, the wrong side for sure! Indeed, neatly folded up at elbow height, the left sleeve this time displays the shiny safety pin! Another luckless one... She sighs with bittersweet relief.

*Engagement Photo, 1944*

*Jacques at 19, a French cadet in training in the U.S. 1945*

*War is over, groom-to-be, October 1945*

*Young bride, February 1946*

# WAITING FOR THE DAY

September 1945 – February 1946

∽

God, how incredibly boring the days had become. Summer would never end. She was convinced of it as she watched the violently colored sunsets promising storms that never came. The parched earth would float around her feet in little cloudbursts of dust whenever she walked on the dirt path along the road, carefully choosing her steps as the weeds on the side had become pricklier, assuming grotesque forms of self-defense against hungry creatures and a leaden sun. The days dragged on. Toward dusk, she was able to note the time by the roars coming from the grounds of the sultan's palace, the high clay red walls visible beyond the wide, open field across from her family's garden. You could set your watch by the sound. At six o'clock on the dot, the lions in their enclosure were being fed some hapless bleating sheep. The noise would soon subside. Its regularity had dulled its meaning, save for the fact that it was six o'clock and close to suppertime.

Once in a while, she wondered about the various goings-on beyond those walls. Whispers persisted from palace suppliers and underlings, horror stories of gothic dimensions specifically centered on the feeding of the animals, stories kept alive by the unapproachable quality of the place. She had thought many times about the women cloistered there, conjuring pictures of *A Thousand and One Nights,* titillating stories of harem life, palace intrigue, and mysterious disappearances.

More often, however, she accepted the distant battlements as part of the landscape, quiet save at feeding time, revealing nothing. A single high gate in the eastern wall would open once a year to let in a rider on a fast horse, his robes flying, holding a headless lamb stretched in front of his saddle in commemoration of Abraham's sacrifice. The immolation took place on the wide field near the wall—the animal had to be presented to the palace with its heart still beating in order to insure good luck to the people.

And good luck was always proclaimed. Still, what did all this have to do with her? She just happened to live there, a young Westerner growing up in a Moslem world, her existence barely touched by these strange customs. Yet, unbeknownst to her, their sights and sounds set a rhythm to her life. Every so often, she would become aware of the melancholy echo of the *muezzin* calling the faithful to evening prayers.

Meanwhile, the days went on, one indistinguishable from the other. Mornings at least held the promise of events bound to happen, a promise heralded by the humming activities of a world slowly awakening as the sun rose. Donkeys skirted the house, laden with goods for the marketplace; endless greetings could be heard from the main road beyond the small field; an ancient and always overloaded bus would grind its gears up the hill toward town. But soon that promise would give way to an acceptance that the coming day would not be any different than the one before, that the sun would beat just as hard, that dusk would bring renewed hunger in men and animals alike, and that no real news would arrive.

The war in Europe was over, finally over. Yet the burst of jubilation at the announcement that peace had come had given way, first to unrealistic expectations, and then to a gradual weariness aggravated by the relentless summer. The soldier she had fallen in love with more than two years before had been lucky, but many would not come back.

She was just marking time. Helping with the household chores under her father's roof, helping her mother tend her younger siblings and neglecting her studies, she had nearly forgotten the wedding dress hanging for years in a closet. Nothing of consequence that she could have undertaken would bear much relevance to her future life, a continent away, and thus she marked the days.

As a child, she'd once been asked by a family friend what she considered to be the best time of her life. It was no doubt an invitation to recount a certain incident from early childhood, filled with wonder and mystery, or the joy of receiving an unexpected gift. She must have surprised the grown-up when she replied in her composed way that that time had not yet come, but she was sure it would happen when she was engaged to be married. She remembered the incredulous laugh her answer brought forth and her embarrassment at sounding so foolish.

"Ah," the person had said, "it's such a short span in one's life, and usually so busy, there's little time left for real happiness."

Now that very time was at hand and how wrong they had both been, the adult no better at predicting than the child. It had been years now since she was spoken for and she still awaited a wedding date. Although thrilling at first with the newness of falling in love with a near stranger, the days since the engagement, concluded by mail, were not short or busy. Her elation had soon been replaced by daily anxieties about his life in a war zone.

With the end of the war, though, real happiness was finally within reach, tantalizingly close. It would come when he'd finally take her away, far, far away. But when she tried to conjure his face, his handsome features blurred, and only a dog-eared photograph could restore them to memory. Because she would be leaving, she looked at her surroundings as if she did not belong there anymore. She now saw her world as strange, inhospitable, and casually cruel; yet she had grown up there. Her detached attitude was a way of preparing herself for the parting from her family. Still, at night, she would cry at the thought of leaving them.

As long as there was no promise of rain in a violent

sky, no news would come; however irrational, she was convinced of this. Some omen had to appear, a sign of change from the clouds or a strong sea breeze or birds…

Finally, one morning she woke up to the smell of damp earth, and when she opened wide the window of her room, dark glistening leaves hung heavy around its frame. As she was sleeping unaware, without fanfare it had rained during the night, the first rain in many months. It must have been a soft, gentle rain since the garden flowers at dawn had merely unfolded their petals to the raindrops still dangling from the trees. The summer cycle was broken at last! Soon the buttercups would crowd the sides of the road and tiny wild iris would pierce through the baked earth in the fields.

The following night, she heard a man sing. She knew who he was: one of the Italian prisoners of war assigned as orderlies to her neighbor, an irascible French officer. She had known about them for some time, a hapless trio of Italian soldiers caught early on in Libya by the Allied forces. They too were waiting for the conflict to be finally over. Once or twice in the beginning, she had caught sight of them as they sneaked by the backyard, and it was explained to her that rules had been bent to let them go to early Mass on Sunday. But people complained: war was war and prisoners were prisoners, and they now had to stay confined within her neighbor's walls, lucky at that to be alive and treated reasonably well. Freedom had not yet come to them. From time to time, fragments of singsong and incomprehensible talk wafted over the high wall separating the houses, confirming their presence. They too had joined the strange backdrop of that eternal summer.

But that night, one of them was singing. The soft rain and now the song: could her waiting be at an end?

It rained again, and this time when the sun returned, it was softer, mistier. The garden had come back to life, and she went outside, delighted by the earthy scents that the rain brought out. An intense sensual feeling of light, smell, and touch nearly overcame her. The lantana bushes exhaled a strong, spicy odor and she found herself kneeling on the damp ground and pressing her face in their blooms.

It was then that she sensed she was being watched. High in a tree beyond the wall was a man. How long had he been there? Rather silly she must have looked, hair over her face, smelling flowers this way and acting the way people did when they thought they were alone. To her own surprise, despite her first reaction to bolt inside, she remained kneeling on the ground and acknowledged his presence with a tentative nod.

He ventured a greeting. *"Buon giorno, signorina."* One of the prisoners... At the tone, she recognized the singer and smiled.

From then on, as each day passed, she found herself waiting for the warm sound of his voice coming over the wall. Something was missing when she did not hear it. She would watch for another glimpse of him. Once she caught him doing the same thing, which embarrassed them both, and another time they met by the neighbor's gate as he and his fellow prisoners worked on the grounds. Pushed forward by his laughing companions, he stood there, hanging his head as she passed by. She sensed it was the closest he had been to a young woman in a long time.

The rain brought cooler days, while the landscape softened into patches of tender green among the thorny bushes. The soft Moroccan winter had settled in. Buttercups and wild marigolds took over the edges of roads and fields. Over the garden trellis, roses were about to bloom. This is when she received the telegram announcing the end of her wait: the near stranger was coming to claim her and the wedding was to be a few short days away. Also her brother should be coming home soon. She recalled the family friend telling her that those days would be hectic, not leaving much time for real happiness. That might have been right after all. Real happiness would come later, to be sure, but she had no time to sort out her feelings, not yet. Now she was being rushed. What irony after all that waiting!

Over the wall, all was quiet. Finally free, the prisoners had just left, heading for home, heading for — what? After an absence of many years from an Italy ravaged by war, they were going home. She was happy for them: she had told him so, when she last saw him along with his fellow prisoners, the singer whose name she never knew.

He had been working on the gravel road leading to their two houses. It was the first time she had talked to him face-to-face, and he responded in earnest. The exchange was awkward since they did not speak each other's language, but for the first time it was free of restraint as they knew they were about to go their separate ways. He somehow conveyed that he wished her happiness on her upcoming marriage. Evidently he had been told the news.

"Ah, you so know?" she said. "He may be here in a few days!"

"Yes," he replied, "that's why we are fixing the road." He pointed at the potholes caused by the rain. "Fixed in time for the wedding, don't worry, *Signorina*," he said, using his hands to make himself understood.

He had looked mildly embarrassed when she burst into sobs. But that had been a few days earlier. Now she was ready for the event.

# A WAR BRIDE'S JOURNEY

## March - April 1946

꙰

I arrived in the United States in the early spring of '46 aboard the ship *Thomas H. Barry*. Formerly a troop carrier, now painted white, she was carrying hundreds of war brides like me to our prospective families. It had been a long trip for the old ship; thanks to the Red Cross's efforts, she had spent a whole month picking up women, from Greece up to the Black Sea, then down to Alexandria and a final stop in Casablanca. The war, finally over a few months earlier, had started just days after my fifteenth birthday. At twenty-one, I was now a married woman.

Many of us had woken up early that raw April morning to catch a glimpse of our new country. We thought we had seen land the night before. A number of women who had been mostly invisible during the trip started to surface on deck. The bedraggled lot, a few of them barefoot, briefly seen when our own group came on board in Casablanca, was finally emerging into the open, many with ill-fitting clothes and borrowed shoes. Despite the many different tongues that separated us, we shared a new pervasive feeling of camaraderie. Each facing a long-awaited day, we stood shivering in the sunless dawn.

The low blackish coastline that might have been a mirage last night was now distinctive. In no time, the land opened up on either side of the ship as we entered a wide channel. Soon, coming from all directions, boats of many shapes and sizes joined us, heading in with us. We passed them one by one as the shores grew closer. From the prow, we suddenly caught sight of the Statue of Liberty, a familiar image to most of us. All its details became sharper to the eye as we glided by. It loomed so big, so green, so close that it jarred the picture I had held in my mind of a statue light and serene holding up her torch in the far distance.

We were still absorbed by the sight when a sailor running by us on the deck pointed to a huge charred hull lying in the middle of the channel. He yelled a word we could not catch at first. Then we understood. It was the *Normandie,* pride of the French before the war, which had met an ignominious end in a fire, tied to her berth in Brooklyn. Aflame, she had been towed out to capsize in deeper water.

I was gazing at the desolate and rusty remains when all of a sudden three light planes swooped down over our ship, then turned around and circled again. The feeling was unnerving. About the same time, tugboats coming out of nowhere took up positions on all sides. Then all hell broke loose. A strange-looking barge started spewing water at us, sirens screamed from land and river, and boat horns blasted. Our ship answered in kind. It was complete pandemonium.

I turned to a steward, yelling at him in my uncertain English: "What is happening?"

He smiled to reassure me. "It's just New York welcoming you."

The moment the sirens stopped, swing music was heard blaring from one of the tugboats. Two gorgeous-looking creatures standing on the back platform next to a loudspeaker started singing toward our ship. They were tall, slender, beautiful, their flowing hair adorned with big white blossoms. They wore fur coats over slinky long dresses, and their bodies moved with the rhythm of their song. I felt a strong kinship with the other women on our boat, so many of us short, ill-dressed, and so inadequate, but yet the brides of returning young soldiers. How could we justify their choice?

The singing stopped suddenly. Our ship was still moving, but very slowly now. From a boat that had pulled alongside, a group of official-looking men holding papers appeared, climbing over the railing, followed by what we guessed from American movies was the press. Scattered around the decks with cards stuck in the ribbons of their wide-brimmed felt hats, a half-dozen reporters tried to corner us into small groups. We shied away as we could not understand the rapid questions thrown at us. Cameras were clicking. I escaped the confusion by fleeing to the bow.

The skyscrapers were now in full view. Still at a

distance, they held no great surprise. Although stunning, they were the New York I expected to find. But the houses closest to the shores on both sides of the river were strange looking. Narrow, stark, and severe in their deep red or gray colors, with evenly spaced windows, equally narrow, without any shutters, they struck me as bleak. Along the drive near the water's edge, humming low, a continuous row of huge cars moved at a rapid pace. The grayness of the landscape was an overwhelming contrast with the land we had last seen over a week earlier. Then, a vibrant sunset had lit the red Moroccan coastline under a cobalt blue sky.

As the boat inched in, the side streets came slowly into focus. They had a tangled look from all the black iron ladders hugging the buildings. Above them, the pale sky merged with the soft outline of that immense city.

I was leaning over the railing when the vibration under my elbows stopped and the faint whirring of the ship came to an end. With the soft prodding of a remaining tugboat, she made a sudden turn on herself. Big cables were thrown overboard. We touched land. We had arrived.

A call from the American consulate two weeks earlier to my family home in Rabat had alerted us that I should leave immediately for Casablanca where a boat was due. Although the war was over and the groom was by then a civilian, due to our very recent marriage

I was classified as a war bride, thus becoming a temporary ward of the American government.

After a particularly tearful farewell with my family in Rabat—since America in those days seemed at the other end of the world—I also had to leave behind my new husband. He would have to find his own transportation due to his new civilian status. Since the war had ended only a few months earlier, means of travel were chaotic and practically nonexistent. But through the consulate, he was notified of a small Liberty ship docked at an Algerian port about to leave for the U.S. the following day. An old captured German relic in the small Rabat airport was the only official air link to Algeria. There was no time to lose. After leaving me with a long final hug at the train station, he would try to hop on it in time to secure passage on the ship.

I cried all the way on the two-hour train ride to Casablanca. Once there, having exhausted my tears, I trudged with my luggage from the station to the specified meeting place at the main market's arcades, crowded as always with Arab rug vendors. A large group of women, some with babies, were already sitting there among bundles and old suitcases. Soon afterwards, a convoy of army buses came to take us to a former high school at the edge of town, a spacious, cheerful-looking place very much like the one I knew in Rabat, and my spirits lifted. Bougainvillea bloomed all over its façade, and in the yard a pleasant breeze greeted us, along with the pungent smell of eucalyptus and pepper trees. Still, the sight of American uniforms everywhere reminded me that we were in an army camp.

We retrieved our belongings and stood waiting for our names to be called. We in the Moroccan contingent were the last group to check in. The day before a trainload of women had arrived from Algeria, many of them after a slow-moving, three-day train ride along the Mediterranean coast. The few we saw looked exhausted, and some babies had taken sick.

We formed a line to be processed. Dog tags with our husband's names were put around our necks. After a light supper that acquainted us with soft white bread, we were assigned to former classrooms in groups of twenty. Cots had been set against walls that still bore blackboards and maps. After chatting a little with my companion on the left, I tried to rest and chase the events of the day from my mind, particularly the look of anguish on my father's face when I had said goodbye. I was about to go to sleep, when all of a sudden a long, loud sob came from nowhere. I froze.

The sobbing continued, becoming even louder. In the short silence that followed, one could feel the tension in the darkness. When the wailing resumed, a soothing voice floated out of the far corner of the room, gradually calming the sobbing girl, still crying, but softly now. More voices joined in.

Between sobs and hiccups, the girl recounted how she had been forced by her family to marry an American G.I., even though she was in love with somebody else. She had been beaten by her father until she gave in. Her Moroccan Jewish family desperately wanted a foothold in America as their life in a Moslem country was difficult. They convinced her it was now or never, and she accepted her part in helping out. But when she tried to say goodbye to the one she loved, her brothers intervened and roughed him up. She could not bear the thought of never seeing him again. Her crying resumed, harsh and desperate.

Soon more sniffling sounds were heard around the room, as if sharing a common sorrow. Darkness had become a comforting and friendly medium. A few talked for a while, until the room became quiet again when sleep took over.

Bright sunshine coming through the curtainless windows greeted us the next morning. We looked at one another, hardly strangers anymore. The crying girl from the night before was recognizable by her doleful look and puffy face. But we had no chance to say much, for soon afterwards loudspeakers started giving orders: first, showers in the gym; then breakfast in another building; and finally a trip to the infirmary. Along with my friendly neighbor from the cot to my left, I went through the various assignments in a fairly lighthearted way. We discovered we had been married on the same day some six weeks earlier. Walking in the courtyard with my new friend in tow, it felt as if I were in school again.

The infirmary was a little alarming, however. Long lines had already formed: we had to have shots. Shots again? A typhus epidemic was ravaging Morocco, but we had all been inoculated. In spite of our vehement protests, we received one more dose plus a series of others. Then, nursing our arms, we were free to return to the shade of the courtyard.

We found the place rife with rumors of mysterious illnesses, sick infants. Would some of the women have to stay behind? We were told that in one room a very frail baby had kept everybody awake all night with his crying, but the army doctor insisted it was just a bad cold and told the mother to stop bothering him. We also heard the ship was approaching Casablanca and would probably dock inside the harbor before dusk. In the far corner of the school grounds, a few of us discovered a small mound and from that vantage point we were able to see the ocean. We looked and looked. At first the horizon appeared quite empty, but then a barely visible but steady white dot was sighted in the distance. We called others to make sure the shimmering lights on the water weren't playing tricks on our eyes. It had to be our boat!

By now the yard was filled with an odd assortment of women, cutting across all strata of the North African population. Their unsophisticated clothing made them look like girls on vacation, except for the young harried mothers among them. There were a few, though, who walked around with an air of assurance and knowhow. They seemed at ease with the American staff and became very valuable in explaining to the rest of us the incomprehensible orders blaring continuously through the loudspeakers.

That afternoon I received a delightful surprise. My name was paged, my new name. After a few seconds of delayed recognition, I hurried to the main building. There, in the lobby, my mother was waiting for me. A compassionate friend had managed to bring her to the camp by car. I was overwhelmed. I brought her out into the schoolyard and we walked arm in arm under the trees, exchanging few words. We were beyond the point of talking. I just needed the soothing warmth of her shoulder against mine, and I cried a bit. Then, too quickly, she had to leave. It was a quiet and tender parting.

As we assembled for the evening meal, the official news came over the intercom: coming from Alexandria, Egypt, the ship was now in the harbor and our departure was set for the following day. Our eyes had not fooled us after all.

The announcement was met with applause and excitement. We checked our heavy luggage and settled in for our last night on shore. Our arms were increasingly sore from the shots and again sleep was hard to come by, but being young we soon gave in. Unlike the night before, our room remained silent.

Just before dawn, we were awakened by running footsteps and voices under our windows. A commotion was heard through the walls. Growing uneasy, we were starting to get up when a woman rushed in and yelled that the sick baby had died. She kept shouting that although several of the women had pleaded with him, the doctor refused to come. He had screamed at them to let him sleep, telling them he had seen the child a few hours earlier and there were no grounds for panic, that they were all hysterical and it was just a bad cold.

*"Can you imagine,"* she yelled at the top of her

voice, *"just a bad cold!"*

Thus a baby died in our midst, his life ebbing away as we slept… We finished dressing with hushed voices, careful not to disturb the disquieting silence in the room next door.

When it's not raining, springtime is beautiful in Morocco. Flowers are at their peak, nights are comfortable, and days are usually clear and warm. It was such a day when we left the camp early that afternoon. Again we formed long lines under a bright sun with our hand luggage at our feet as a column of tarpaulin-covered trucks waited to take us to the harbor a few miles away. After each vehicle was filled, a soldier sat on the floor, his back turned away from us, blocking the rear opening. We took off.

By the time the trucks finally slowed to a halt, the heat under the tarp was unbearable. From our benches on either side of the truck, we could see a boat hull through the rear. Our guard, with his back turned and feet dangling outside, yelled at us to stay seated.

I felt faint from the stifling heat and grabbed the hand of the girl next to me. She begged the guard to let me out. Chewing gum, he shrugged his shoulders and shook his head without looking at us. I directed the anger mounting in my throat at the back of his neck. Then, gasping for air, I gave up. Various hands grabbed me as I slumped forward.

When I came to, it was pure heaven: I was outside, smelling salty air. Just in front of the truck, looming huge and white with a big Red Cross emblem, was the ship that had come for us.

❦

The large cabin was cramped with tired and confused women, crying babies, and luggage. I set my belongings on the berth assigned me and rushed back up into the fresh air, yearning for a little solitude. Sitting against the railing, I rested and watched the last formalities of a ship heading out to sea.

From childhood, I had always found fascinating the sight of cargo being lifted by a crane and hanging precariously over the hold before disappearing into the ship's bowels. Whenever our family had occasion to sail to France before the war, I would stay on deck to watch the final preparations, hoping to catch a glimpse of some passenger rushing on board just seconds before the link to shore was cut.

I was not to be disappointed on this trip. Strange-looking packages, many wrapped in rugs and held together with ropes, were scooped up and dropped into the gaping hole. Then a last passenger came running up the gangplank as it was lifted away, a blondish woman who looked a little older than most of us. She was laughing and panting at the same time, her veiled white hat askew, a big corsage on her shoulder, and very visibly pregnant.

"I made it, I made it!" she kept saying to no one in particular. As soon as she reached the deck, she started waving wildly to a group that had gathered down below on the wharf. The men, evidently members of a wedding party, were wearing white carnations in their lapels. They yelled to her, cupping their hands so she could hear them and jovially slapping one another on the back.

The boat was ready to leave. Nothing any longer connected us to land. After blowing a few last kisses toward shore, the new bride sighed with relief and collapsed happily on a deck chair. She straightened her hat and pushed the veil back from her face. Congratulated by fellow passengers on deck who had witnessed her arrival, she became a little wistful. The whole scene had a comical overtone, lightening the tension of the moment.

Slowly the boat angled away from the wharf. I was relieved that the faces ashore were unknown to me. I could not have withstood the gradual dimming of loved ones' features into nothingness. As a child, I had watched my grandmother standing by herself on a French shore, a tiny figure on the dock waving goodbye to us with her handkerchief until she blended into the crowd behind her, becoming nothing more than a white dot as the space between us grew.

The Casablanca harbor was like a maze and the boat moved at a crawl, navigating around rusty, half-sunk hulls, some barely breaking the surface. Finally, all of a sudden, we were out in the open. A strong breeze greeted us, lifting skirts, blowing our long hair over our faces. Most of the women scurried below deck. It was not quite dusk and the sky had become flamboyant, the setting sun bringing out strong hues from the land, while the ocean took on a deep emerald color, the propeller lightening the water into a pale undercurrent crowned with foam.

Slowly I made my way toward the deserted stern.

The ship's wake stretched behind us in a wide arc. Leaning on the railing, I could now see the sprawling city of Casablanca in its entirety, from the hills of Anfa down to the harbor. It looked very white and peaceful. Then the distance and declining rays of the sun gave it a pinkish cast, until it collapsed from view.

We did not lose sight of the red and rocky coast for a while. Over there, to the north, was my home, the family I had left behind. Did they sense that I was within sight? It was time for the evening meal and I pictured them around the table, all unusually quiet, even my younger siblings. Could they guess how close I was?

But now the stretch of water between the boat and land was widening. Over there were the beaches, the tidal pools, the rocky crevices I knew so well. Yet, viewed from sea, the coastline looked unfamiliar, almost inhospitable. For an instant, the shore lit up as the sun's last rays touched it over the darkening waters.

Good riddance! I suddenly felt rebellious: there was a new life ahead of me! I did not care if I ever saw that country again, with all its miseries of late, its long dry spells, its epidemics, its suffering natives; all the people I knew who had not come home from the war and would never come back, despite the wild hopes of their loved ones. It was a beautiful country, but too harsh, too harsh, unlike my native land. Still I stood there, transfixed, watching the shores disappear.

I heard a woman crying. I was not alone. Turning, I recognized her by the silent companions standing nearby as the mother who had lost her baby early that morning. Her tears flowed unchecked as, head in hands, she looked back at the shore now reduced to a thin black line on the horizon. We had been told the child's body had to be left behind.

Darkness fell soon upon us, and the wind picked up. A gong sounded: it was time to go inside.

The next morning found our ship moving full steam ahead on a quiet sea. The sky was not as bright as on land. In chairs scattered about the upper deck, a number of us enjoyed the sun's warmth while watching the clear horizon slowly lift and dip with the ship's motion. Swing music blared from one of the sitting rooms; we could have been on a cruise.

But confusion still reigned. At daybreak, I answered the wrong bell and found myself sharing a breakfast table with a group of women who might have been Polish or Romanian. A number of Eastern Europeans were on board. They tried several languages on me before finally giving up. We smiled a lot, and they giggled among themselves at my bewilderment and giggled more on discovering I was French, which matter was settled with a few German words. All were rather thin and shabbily dressed. One was barefoot although it was scarcely winter's end. I quickly returned to my own group: at least we spoke the same tongue. We were called for drill practice up on deck and given life preservers, followed by several orders.

"*Qu'est-ce-qu'ils disent?*" What are they saying? We

strained to understand the Red Cross officials.

"No fraternizing with the crew, no climbing up in the lifeboats…" The list went on. It was only a matter of time before most rules would be broken. One of the most demure and elegant girls on the ship, a colonel's wife who had come on board with a veiled blue hat and stunning outfit to match, climbed on top of a lifeboat soon afterwards and performed a belly dance to the delight of crew and passengers alike. It was even whispered that the officer on night duty had a few surprises when lifting the canvas on some lifeboats. As a result, there were sailors confined to the brig for the trip's duration. Gossip became our main entertainment.

On deck that first morning at sea, good humor abounded. The pain of parting belonged to the day before. In the cabins below were still some sick and tired girls, young mothers and those still grieving. Yet up in the fresh air, a general sense of relief took over. Free from the hardships brought by war, real adventure lay ahead with a companion, a husband we hardly knew, in settings we could only imagine. Though mixed with anxiety, the feeling of bursting out in such a new direction was most welcome.

After announcing ship regulations, the Red Cross officials disappeared and we were left to enjoy long hours in the sun, acquainting ourselves and comparing stories. Slowly we made friends while watching an incredibly empty ocean. It was hard to imagine the sea could be so quiet and peaceful.

A small and very beautiful young woman with a thick blond braid to her knees came up late that morning with a retinue. Rumors flew about her: she was a Greek from Cairo and her wedding two months earlier had been a big event, her father being extremely wealthy. Conscious of the stares she attracted, she loosened her hair, which in the wind cascaded down around her. One of her attendants smoothed it away from her face. Accepting the attention as natural, she appeared a lovely spoilt child. How would life in America treat her?

It was a time for confidences, but my own shyness made me a listener. I tagged along with my friend from camp to visit and help a few women who had chosen to stay below. One was already a widow. We found the girl, who did not look over eighteen, dressed in drab colors, sitting quietly on her bunk. My friend, an inexhaustible gossip, had told me earlier that shortly after their one-day honeymoon her husband had been killed in action. Her hands in her lap, the girl answered our questions in an odd, flat voice: Why was she going? Well, her mother-in-law wanted it. They had a farm and he was her only son… We asked her to join us for some fresh air on the deck. Wrapped in widowhood, she shook her head.

Continuing our tour, we discovered that the distraught woman who had cried so hard that first night in camp was in sick bay and we secured permission to see her. Ill luck seemed to pursue the girl. She lay very pale on her narrow hospital cot, resigned to her fate or too sick to care. She had just been told she had syphilis and would be quarantined on arrival at Ellis Island, probably sent back. Her family, for all their efforts, might never make it to the States after all. She imparted the shocking news in a detached way, showing bitterness only toward her unloved husband for putting her in that state. She was mostly in dread of the painful injections inflicted on her poor body every few hours. We promised to return, but we were dismayed. To my shame, upon leaving I refrained from touching her.

Soon afterwards, the weather changed. Both sky and sea turned gray. The dip and lift of the ship, so gentle at first, became more pronounced. Lying in my berth that night, my head close to the wall, I could hear cracking sounds, then ominous silences followed by a long shudder and finally a rending noise as if the ship were breaking in two. The babies in our cabin grew restless and cried fitfully throughout the night.

At daybreak, I escaped the stuffy confines of our cabin, hanging tightly onto brass railings while making my way to higher levels. Most of the heavy doors to the deck were secured shut, but one had swung wide open under pressure from the wind. I ventured out. Swept with salty sprays, the decks were very slippery. I braced myself in an outside stairway and breathed deeply the cold fresh air that came in violent spurts. Two other women joined me. We formed a chain, linking arms, and tried to walk. The wet gusts slapped and stung our faces. We loved it. But it was foolhardy, and with some reluctance we retreated to the warm but uncomfortable security of the main sitting room.

The storm worsened by the hour and many women became sick. For most, this was their first experience at sea, and they were frightened. Loudly, lyrically, they started to berate their absent husbands. Curses with Mediterranean flavor and imagery were invoked against uncaring men who presently stood no chance of being forgiven, ever. But where was my own new husband in that storm? Liberty ships were so small. How was he faring?

Down in our cabin, the air was foul, as the babies were not being properly tended by their seasick mothers. My offer of help was accepted with indifference, and the stench finally drove me out.

As I walked to the upper level holding onto railings, I heard some music. Following the sounds, I discovered the movie projection room. Greer Garson and Walter Pidgeon were about to entertain the audience in the new Hollywood war picture *Mrs. Miniver,* showing England in her finest hour.

The film was pleasing to the eye and Greer was lovely and elegant. I was most envious of her pale, flawless complexion. The onscreen dialogue was difficult to follow and became even more so as the first signs of seasickness came on. I tried to focus on the green and tender colors of the English landscape, but sensed that they would lead to the darkening clouds of war. Outside the storm was raging. Movie explosions started to blend with the moans of our ship. Chairs in the room slipped and slid amidst loud crashes. Nausea finally gripped my throat and I succumbed, thus missing the film's end. I was taken back to the cabin where I was strapped to my berth by two men who happened to be in the audience. What were they doing on board? Back from some secret missions, was the rumor. Why were they here and not my husband? Why were we separated? But seasickness has a way of obliterating everything else, and I gradually fell asleep.

The storm lasted three long days and nights. Though the sea eventually calmed, the skies stayed dark over leaden waters. Stalled by the worst part of the gale in the mid-Atlantic, the ship was now slowly approaching American shores. Soon, radio messages arrived from land. Answering wires sent by the Red Cross about our impending arrival, families were extending greetings to their new daughters-in-law from their homes in various parts of the country. I heard my name over the loudspeakers. It was a telegram with words of welcome from my new family. This tenuous link with Michigan, my future home, buoyed my spirits. Still, for many of my companions, an ominous silence persisted.

Late that afternoon, seagulls appeared around the ship, seagulls from the New World! They dove into our wake and then swooped over the deck just as the pregnant middle-aged bride emerged from below. She looked wan and even thinner, but her face lit up at the sight. Still wearing the same hat, but without the veil, she greeted the women on deck like long-lost friends, vowing to all who could hear that she would show California, her destination, what Parisian chic was all about.

At dinnertime it was announced we would arrive early the next morning. And we did. We finally welcomed New York, and New York welcomed us with big fanfare and then some.

As soon as we touched land, a string of military police came on board and positioned themselves on the decks. On previous arrivals, a few women had jumped ship and disappeared without a trace. This time we would be watched until we had been securely transferred.

Soon after, a string of families came on board to claim their new relatives, and the appropriate brides were paged. From a balcony overlooking the reception room, I watched as they waited below, pale and fidgety with apprehension, in a scene resembling a modern slave auction. I felt my heart pound. A few had faded tattoos on their foreheads and chins, marking their North African ancestry. If there was disappointment on either side, it did not show at that moment. Suddenly there erupted a shout of joy. Among us was a lone "male war bride"—a movie would be made later with that title—and his wife had come to claim him with a few boisterous friends. The reunion made the *New York Times* front page the next morning. We were big news.

Wistfully we waived to our departing shipmates as they reached the wharf below, leaving one by one with their worldly possessions. Following someone in charge, they disappeared into Customs, swallowed into the mysteries of another world.

By the time evening fell that first night, families had stopped coming. Although I did not really expect it, I too had held out hope that my husband might be there waiting for me. But for many, there were no signs of welcome at all, no wires, letters, or calls.

Then the loudspeaker announced a few days' wait on board for the rest of us until train reservations could be secured. Apart from the police still watching us on the decks and in corridors, we were left to ourselves. We had no idea what had happened to the woman in sick bay. I started scribbling a letter to my family in Morocco…

The mood on the ship changed quickly. With nothing to do, a roving group of streetwise women banded together. They felt they had been snubbed by "uppity" women pulling rank on them during the trip and they were going to get even. One never knew when the threats would no longer be verbal. Yet they seemed to be on the best of terms with the men watching us.

The second night after our arrival, a woman threw herself overboard. She had just received word her husband's family did not want her as they had no room for her. As she was fished out of the dirty water unharmed, somebody said she looked like a half-drowned cat.

Little by little each day, friends made on board were leaving. The days stretched into a full week during which we were transferred from our gleaming white Red Cross ship to a worn-out troop carrier in the berth next to ours, joining stranded war brides from England. We were all confused about what would happen next. We could only guess that the Red Cross was encountering bureaucratic tangles as many soldiers were coming home at the same time. The excitement we had felt upon our arrival quickly died down since we were not allowed to set foot on shore. We were also enjoined to keep our dog tags around our necks at all times.

Time crawled ever so slowly on the troopship. Warehouses hid the streets and all we could take in were the skyscrapers' outlines and muffled city noises. We watched with envy the few people allowed to disembark. We had plenty of time to write families back home, trusting that someone would mail our letters. I later learned they were never received.

Then came Easter Sunday! That day, I literally set foot on American soil. An ecumenical chaplain led a service in the ship's mess hall and afterwards it was announced that buses would take us on a tour.

It was a bright and sunny day, although cool for those of us from warmer climates. Half a dozen buses lined up along the wharf. After more than two weeks on board ship, it was finally our turn to walk down the gangplank and touch firm soil. Minutes later, our caravan started and soon we were in the middle of Manhattan, twisting our necks at the dizzying skyscrapers glimpsed through the bus windows. The traffic was intense and soon slowed to a crawl. We had a chance to examine the throngs of people ambling on the sidewalks, all well-dressed in colorful clothes. This was a spectacle hard to imagine, except perhaps in movies. Our tour guide explained it was the Easter Parade on Fifth Avenue. We had never heard the term before. We saw tall beautiful women wearing floppy hats crowned with roses as big as cabbages. Others just had white flowers over their ears. Corsages abounded. The sight was incredible, like a moving garden in bloom. Lucky us to join this world!

The buses picked up speed and we crossed a bridge. It was announced that the Bronx Zoo was next. I can't remember much about the animals, but retain a vivid memory of one open and hilly place between cages where the grass was an unusually tender green under a pale blue sky. It was a wonderful feeling to walk along a path with real dirt under our feet, even if still in supervised groups. We drew curious stares from other zoo visitors. We must have been an odd-looking bunch, more like young women from a detention home. But we too studied them: these were real people, real families, real children. In time, we would be them.

Finally, the day came when it was my turn to leave, along with a few of my North African companions. Dusk was falling when we joined half a dozen English brides in the cavernous Grand Central Station. They were warm, friendly, and efficient. Together, we formed the Michigan contingent.

The night on the train went by quickly in a congenial atmosphere as we laughed together at the odd contraptions of Pullman bunks. The British girls admired our suntans, declared them "super," and we envied their ease with the language. We slept little as we kept peering through the windows. It was too dark to decipher much of the countryside, and whenever the train slowed down we could see only bleak successions of warehouses. Spring had yet to reach this part of the world.

As the night wore on, we nervously promised to stay in touch, perhaps form a group to help one another, and exchanged addresses. A gray dawn greeted us when the train finally stopped and our names were called out for the last time. We ventured slowly down the steps, hair in place, hearts beating. We had been ready for hours.

Small clusters of people were waiting on the platform. There was hesitation on both sides, scanning for faces familiar from photographs. All of a sudden, hugs and exclamations surrounded and separated us. Two eager, good-looking women claimed me as their new sister and led me to a tall older man who kissed me on the forehead as a sign of welcome. My traveling companions had vanished. I was led to a car where a very elderly person was waiting, my husband's grandmother. I was now on my own among a new family. My voyage was over.

A week later, a Liberty ship among many others slid into New York Harbor with the groom on board. The following morning at the railway station in Detroit, I flew into his arms.

*Thomas H. Barry, war bride ship*